Making Believers

Connect to the Light within...

LINDA AMATO

BALBOA.
PRESS

A DIVISION OF HAY HOUSE

Balboa Press books may be ordered through booksellers or by contacting:

Balboa Press
A Division of Hay House
1663 Liberty Drive
Bloomington, IN 47403
www.balboapress.com
1-(877) 407-4847

Because of the dynamic nature of the Internet, any web addresses or links contained in
this book may have changed since publication and may no longer be valid. The views
expressed in this work are solely those of the author and do not necessarily reflect the
views of the publisher, and the publisher hereby disclaims any responsibility for them.

The author of this book does not dispense medical advice or prescribe the use
of any technique as a form of treatment for physical, emotional, or medical
problems without the advice of a physician, either directly or indirectly. The
intent of the author is only to offer information of a general nature to help you
in your quest for emotional and spiritual well-being. In the event you use any
of the information in this book for yourself, which is your constitutional right,
the author and the publisher assume no responsibility for your actions.

Any people depicted in stock imagery provided by Thinkstock are models,
and such images are being used for illustrative purposes only.
Certain stock imagery © Thinkstock.

Printed in the United States of America

ISBN: 978-1-4525-3543-2 (sc)
ISBN: 978-1-4525-3545-6 (hc)
ISBN: 978-1-4525-3544-9 (e)

Library of Congress Control Number: 2011909219

Balboa Press rev. date: 07/11/2011

For My Dad
Edward A. Symanski

"You are the wisest man I ever met…"

For My Soul Sister and Muse
Pat Roperto

"Your encouragement and faith in me made me a believer…"

Gratitude

I would like to begin my gratitude page by expressing how grateful and thankful I am to God for this life experience and bringing Gracie and Amanda into my consciousness, as well as making my dreams come true...

My parents, I will love you both always, and although my dad has moved on, I am amazed at all that you shared with me, and I will forever treasure our talks. Mom, you are gentle and eternally young in my eyes...

As well as being the best spiritual/human teacher I could ever ask for, my husband has been my best friend, lover, and confidant during many happy and sad moments all of these years. Mostly, I love him for his strength and thank him for loving my dad...

Where would I be without Tory, Tina, Nicholas, and Jess? You allowed me to be the best mother by pushing me to my limits but by also showing me not to be so serious – that all is well in the end! I am proud to be your mother and friend...

Lisa, we had to be soul sisters in a past life. I am very happy that you are part of this family...

My grandsons, Hunter and Hudson, my love overflows for the chance to be the best for you guys. Truly I am blessed to be your LA-LA...

My family and friends from yesterday, I have learned from you all. We have laughed together and cried together, but the life experience we shared has allowed me to transform to be a better me…

There are many new people in my life that have lighted my path by their own glow from within…these are my Spiritual Teachers that have written all the books I have read as if they were textbooks that I must learn from, especially all of the Hay House authors. Louise L. Hay was the first to open my mind to the power of my thoughts; I am eternally grateful to her…

Monica Keano, who taught me to be a Reiki Master, led me to the Institute for Integrative Nutrition to be a Certified Holistic Health Counselor and empowered me to believe in myself which led me to opening my own business, Believable Alternatives, and in doing so, I follow her example as my mentor to mentor others.

Joshua Rosenthal, the Founder of the Institute for Integrative Nutrition, what a profound teaching experience you offered, and I must say I use everything you taught me to make a difference during this life experience.

Hugs to my clients who have helped me during my own transition into Plan "B" by sharing with me so that I could empower and fall in love with them! I appreciate every moment we share…

Heartfelt thanks to Joan, Courtney, Brandon and Valerie at Balboa Press. It has been an enjoyable experience working with them. They have been very encouraging, supportive and a pleasure to work with.

With Love and Light, LA

Contents

Introduction

I have been having a human experience that has led me to my spiritual journey for some years now, and I hope that my story fills you with insight and clarity that will lead you to believe.

I almost laughed out loud when I wrote "a spiritual journey." Truly, I believe that I am a Spiritual Being having a human experience, which was the first thought process that was new that I have learned during these past years.

This story is a fictional, non-fictionalized account of many women's lives. I felt the need to share this story because I am amazed that this story can be true for anyone who has experienced fear, guilt, shame, grief, lies, illusion, attachment, despair, or low self-esteem. As a daughter of an alcoholic, manic-depressive parent who labeled me "author," I could not not write this book. After all, I promised that I would.

I am married to my childhood boyfriend for the last 40 years, and we have had our fears and tears, being that we raised one another. What could we have known when we left our parents' homes to start a home of our own at such a young age? I had my experiences, and he had his, and we brought them into our marriage. The invisible thread of love we share for one another allowed us to be tied together forever and to never give up on one another.

Learning that we are raised by parents that were raised by parents that were raised by parents and on and on as it goes taught me to look within to what mattered to me most. As a young mother, I knew what kind of parent I wanted to be, and I dedicated myself to my children. I learned from them that unconditional love is the key to a child growing up.

In this story, that is something Gracie and Amanda strive to find but never expected to find it from one another. Gracie and Amanda struggle with verbal and mental abuse that takes them to the pits of despair – something once again, that many women can relate to. I can list many who have spoken to me in a negative, hateful, racist manner. But, that is not part of the story.

Life is great and filled with miracles and an abundance that many of us do not believe. Hopefully, you will be witness to how great life can be even if it is not the life you had imagined.

In Book One, "The Mansions of the Mind," I offer you a look into the mind of a mentally ill, alcoholic parent. In Book Two, "The Passions of the Mind," I take you on a journey that change and transformation of the self is possible when one believes in many different avenues and is bold and courageous enough to go for it. To simply go with the flow is the greatest of lessons I have been able to learn.

Gracie and Amanda are a combination of my own soul and that which I have searched for most of my adult life. It is the discovery that love is the glue to any life and all that matters in the end.

A look within and being able to hear the voice of your soul will enable you, my reader, to transform your own life and become a believer that anything is possible.

I believe that there is a Gracie and Amanda inside of us all and that we hide behind the masks of our daily existence. However, Amanda shows that transformation, change, growth, and expansion of the self are possible for everyone.

With Love, Light, and Hugs, LA

BOOK ONE / PLAN "A"

The Mansions of the Mind

In this story, you will meet Gracie Jewel and me, her daughter Amanda. Gracie escapes into the mansions of the mind, as she calls it, as a woman searching for love most of her life. I will leave it up to you if you think she is manic-depressive, as society labeled her for the last thirty years of her life.

For some reason she cannot comprehend, Gracie cannot get a grasp on her life. She started very young not being able to experience a feeling of being loved. In reality she is betrayed by all who come into her life, but one.

Gracie's favorite saying was always "that she could have been a contender." She loved movies, ice cream, and chocolate. Somehow along the way she needed to escape and she found the solution to living a life by accepting her life. As her daughter I believed her to be very wise, and in the mansions of the mind, I hope I am able to portray how special I felt she was in her own way.

It is not easy for a child to be witness to alcoholism, abuse, and feel fear in the pit of the stomach. Still, I never held anything against Gracie because unconditionally I loved her. I truly did not think that anything was her fault. There was a time I blamed most of everything on my father. However, this is not a story about him. Making Believers is a story about my mom, Gracie Jewel.

Chapter One

Fear

Amanda noticed that she was trembling as she stood in her mother's empty room. She turned around slowly, trying to imagine living like this for an entire life. Confused, sad, and hurt she let the tears fall. She sat on the bed and cried for the loss of her mom. She was filled with an ache inside her heart. Pain that she never realized she would ever have. Her life today at this moment seemed upside down and inside out. A jumbled mess that had come to a screaming halt!

She hated coming to visit her mother all of these years. Fear stayed with her as the nightmares came. The smell of sick, dirty adults and the cries and sounds of unloved people tormented her. Through the years though, she could not not come. After all, Gracie was her mom. In her own way she loved her craziness too. She found her to be wise in her knowledge and beliefs. Just to accept to live in this world for thirty years considered by society and doctors as a mentally ill person had to stand for something. This belief even at times amazed Gracie. Amanda didn't visit because she was her mother. She visited her because she was a human being that was hurting and in search of love. Amanda didn't love her because she was her mother solely; she loved her because she simply could not. The mother part and the daughter part they fell into through the years.

Amanda never feared like her brother that she too would become sick in her mind. This was because she didn't believe Gracie was sick. Gracie simply loved too deeply. She believed in God and she showed and taught Amanda to love unconditionally. Her reason for being was love in her life, truly, madly, and deeply.

With the back of her hand and sleeve from her shirt Amanda wiped the tears from her face. A smile slowly fell onto her lips from within. The hours she had spent talking and discussing life with her mother was beyond normal. Their belief always was that God gave only each of us what we could handle in life. There was actually a reason for everything in life. Life was a test Gracie taught her, and in the end she would pass because she had Gracie as her teacher.

She glanced towards the dresser and saw something yellow. The two top drawers were empty. At the bottom she found a stack of papers inside an envelope tied with a yellow ribbon and a crumbled-up picture. On a piece of paper she recognized her mother's shaky handwriting. She had written, "SAVE ALL MY WRITINGS! A BOOK IS IN THE MAKING THROUGH MY DAUGHTER." Amanda trembled as she hugged the papers to her chest. She sobbed for herself because she knew down deep that Gracie was at peace.

She placed the envelope in a bag that was empty as well, for there was nothing of Gracie for her to take except this envelope. It seemed that Gracie had left her a "gift." One final look around the room and she closed the door and left. A part of her was aware that she was stepping now onto a new path in life. She realized that her life was to be quite different without Gracie in it. How she would react to this change and accept what was expected of her she would learn eventually.

The memories she had collected throughout the years were like photographs in her mind. Amazingly she was not even surprised to learn that Gracie believed she was capable of writing a book. This had always been her dream and Gracie actually introduced her to people as "her daughter, the author." For years Amanda wrote poetry and little stories but she never believed she was good enough to actually write an entire book. Growing up in a home that was torn and empty turned her towards the written word. An avid reader she toyed with writing as a release of her own fears. To be afraid all of these years that she was not educated enough to ever accomplish her own dream to become a published author. Now Gracie leaves her a note with some papers stating she is to write a book. Amanda smiles and thinks that Gracie is definitely laughing at her now.

Once in the car she just sits and feels the heat of the sun on her face. Her body shakes as she sobs at the realization that life will be without Gracie. How does she accomplish continuing on without her? For years they had spent hours together just talking. No one ever knew the Gracie that she did and she believed no one would cry for her either. For the loss of a life that was confused, misjudged, in search of love, and labeled by society today filled her with pain. This was the truth of life that saddened Amanda the most. A mere fact that was true, Gracie had been alone in life except for her.

Amanda believed that she would never feel as special as Gracie had made her believe she was. The shedding of tears will be for her because she had no regrets or guilt. She knew in her heart she had been a great daughter. As a child of a mentally ill parent she accepted life always and never was embarrassed of who she was. She was never embarrassed by Gracie or felt that she could harm her in any way. She accepted Gracie, as long as she could remember, as just being her mom. She was not aware of what they call today a dysfunctional household. She felt love and experienced sadness growing up and accepted that this was life. She knew of no other way to be. Growing up she learned that no one deserved to be alone or forgotten about. The truth about Amanda was that she, like Gracie, loved deeply.

Her mind was swirling around with the past and the years of spending time with Gracie. The many laughs they enjoyed even while she was institutionalized. Visiting her Amanda became aware of the abuse and neglect in our society. The forgotten lives that she imagined children lived through like her but could not cope with the pressures of seeing their parent ill. To Amanda life was about the journey and what one can learn. The choices we get to make daily. She could have chosen to walk away from Gracie but she would not be able to live with herself. She had memories of Gracie not being ill and looking up to her with the eyes of a loving child. The hardest part for her now will be to accept that she has a life of her own to live.

Amanda calmed herself with a silent prayer to the Blessed Mother to give her the strength to do what is expected of her. The next few days will be about planning her funeral, then she will sit and read Gracie's words. At this time her heart deeply ached and she knew it was not the time to look into the precious "gift" she had been left. There were arrangements to be made for the final goodbye to be given.

Gracie's body lay now in a sealed coffin. The funeral home was packed, full of people who did not know Gracie. There were a handful of close family that years ago were part of Gracie's life. The rest were friends of Amanda, her husband, and children. Respect for her loss on their faces and in their whispers to each other, today they offered time, prayer, and flowers to console her in the loss of this woman that they had never met. Everyone heard of Gracie at one time or another only because of the curiosity of a parent being mentally ill and institutionalized. It almost could make someone famous! Amanda was silent and calm as she looked around and wondered what Gracie would be thinking.

Gracie would chuckle and be proud that Amanda knew so many people. That she lived a life that Gracie always craved. Last night her father had called and asked if she needed him there. He felt since he was remarried that he would be out of place. At first Amanda was shocked; then she realized that she didn't want him there either. It was better only because for thirty years he had nothing to do with Gracie. People would hug him and comfort him at the loss of his wife, only because he was Amanda's father. A long time ago she had accepted that he had made a new life for himself. She knew about the pain and guilt that one feels from betrayal and he had to live his life with what he had done in the past to Gracie. It didn't matter that Gracie was dead because his nightmares were not. In the end, Amanda believed that Gracie was a much better human being than her father because she was capable of forgiveness.

As she knelt in front of the coffin to say her final goodbye, she realized she did not know how to say this. Fear gripped her throat and heart as the thoughts attacked her mind. Did she forget to tell her she loved her? Maybe she could have gotten another opinion from other doctors? If only she had listened to Amanda and lived with her! The biggest question was that she was really gone now. That is the realization that haunted Amanda and brought sadness into her existence that she feared the most.

As she looked around at her own children's tears at the cemetery, she felt proud that they loved their grandmother. Through the years they accepted Gracie and wondered like her if she was really ill. Would life for everyone now return to normal after the burial? Amanda believed no one would be as affected as she by the death of her mom. She felt scared of tomorrow and existing in this life without Gracie. An emptiness inside that she never realized would be there now suffocated her. There was no relief in Gracie's death for her.

It was evening now and her house was silent and still. A different life would present itself in the morning. She knew it would be a life without Gracie, mentally ill people, institutions, and doctors from now on. A life without a mother!

A pain in her heart awakens her again as it has for the past three months. She feels foggy as if she is forgetting something. She remembers this feeling and calls it the memory of death. She does not want to rise but knows she must. She sits at the table with a hot cup of coffee remembering Gracie. Her thoughts are stumbling all over the place requiring that she recall every detail. She is afraid of moving forward and forgetting. Her feelings are exposed on her face and in her eyes for all to witness. She laughs out loud as she wonders if it is possible for one to crack under the pressure of death.

The sun warms her face as she tries to begin her day. Like a vice her heart is gripped by the knowledge that Gracie is gone. She knew she was dying but she still was not prepared for this feeling inside. Why is it so hard to say goodbye? Through the years she wrote poetry to ease her own troubled mind. A release of her fears that would be put on paper as a confession and belief. For when these words would be read later Amanda would realize the strength and comfort she found in them. A journal and pen worked wonders in her life as a companion and tools to live by. She notices that her face is wet and tears are falling from her eyes. She opens her journal and there on the first page is a poem she had written four months ago. It is like seeing into her mind and reading her fears. She cannot remember writing this poem but that happens most of the time to her. She has journals upstairs and downstairs in her car and jots down simple words from her heart whenever she can. When she opens a journal and comes across her own words she is surprised and believes: wow, I guess that is how I felt back then. Unfortunately, she does not have that feeling upon reading this poem and struggles with reading her own words. Ironic, she thinks to herself, as she begins to read the title with a tear in her eye.

I Don't Know How to Say Goodbye

She comes into my dreams at night, a woman I loved all my life.
Fear fills my mind, even though I know she is kind.
Sweat on my brow from the night, I awaken ready for a fight.
Confused and angry I cry for the need to understand, so I try.
To come to terms with her fate, the unknown is what I hate.
These nights are turbulent and long, tossing
and turning I am no longer strong.
I pretend during the day to be all right!
Even though I know fear will come in the night.
A woman I loved all my life awaits the Angel of Death to appear.
I wonder if she is filled with fear.

Amanda paces back and forth in her kitchen thinking how powerful her own words are. She will begin with this poem. She sits down and turning the page begins to share her emotions from the depths of her soul.

I learned to show no pain. I can hide the sorrow within. No one can hear my thoughts. My feelings belong to me. I do not need to share them with anyone. I feel as if I am in a moment that I cannot escape. I see the world moving forward, but I do not comprehend how to move with it. I am strong and I shall ease myself out somehow. I need time to sit and think. It seems as if I am about to fall off a cliff but something always makes me not plunge forward. I amaze myself at the ability I have to draw strength to live on in this world filled with pain.

The pain is the strongest at night. In the darkness, as the tears fall, no one sees. No one can hear me sob. I might be having a nervous breakdown, I think to myself. Yet, no one is aware that I suffer. I lay for hours in my bed at night as I pray the rosary to distract my mind and search for peace. If I close my eyes tightly I picture God above me guiding me through the night. There is a whisper of a voice in my head, "I can do this." I toss and turn constantly, wanting to dream of happy times, but nightmares come instead.

During the day a black cloud hangs overhead, waiting for me to arrive, waiting and watching from above. I feel there is no escape from this black cloud. If I were to go into the cloud my pain will be there for all to see. Their response will be that she's having a difficult time. All around me they will become uncomfortable and I know the questions I would be asked: "What's wrong with you? Can't you get on with your life? Are you that depressed? You are not acting yourself, why?" I can answer all the questions with four words, "My heart is broken." If I was no longer capable of hiding the pain, then I will be considered weak. A person who is not strong and not able to get on with her life!

I am not asking for years or just a few more months, maybe a day or two more, possibly a week longer is what is needed to heal my sorrow. How do I start to cry and shed this pain through my tears? How do I show that I suffer within? How do I make them understand? I feel in my heart that I need time. The problem is, I don't know how much time I need. Does anybody know how much time is needed to say "goodbye?"

I function daily but it is a struggle. I must go on, I tell myself. I push forward because of the responsibilities of my life. To give up would be too easy. To stop my thoughts is what I desire. How does one shut off their mind? If I can capture the pain and sorrow and place it on paper with my blood as the ink, I believe I shall escape. I can then say, "Read my pain, touch my words that came from my mind, now do you understand?" I doubt they will. I want silence in the world around me. I want to stay in this moment and feel my pain. I want to hurt. I believe if I get the chance to feel the pain and bleed, then I can be cured with the healing of my purpose in life as my band-aid.

I have a job to do as a wife and a mother. I just need time to sit back and contemplate this change, for it shall be different from now on. I have pushed the pain to the darkest corners of my soul but it sits waiting for me. This loss that will last forever has awakened me to reflect on the world all around. No one really cares, why? Many titles I carry and some have now been erased because of death, and this I feel is my greatest loss. In reality, I am not alone for there are people all around me who mean well but do not understand. I have my husband and children. I have my friends and people I work with. My pain has not affected their world. My sorrow lies within me and I have learned to hide it well. The realization that life does go on is the saddest part. To love and then hurt from loss has to be the hardest experience of life.

This pain I speak of for this woman that I loved that is now gone fills me totally. I need her to sit with, to talk to, and to laugh with. I find it sad that I alone feel this inner pain because she is no longer. Maybe that is why I want to scream for her to come back to me. She belonged to me in many ways; most importantly she was my friend. In reality I have lost more than one person with her death. I cry for me not her. I know she is at peace and I need to find mine. I thought I was prepared, I saw it coming, the cancer eating her spirit, stealing her laughter, changing her before my eyes. The open sore in my heart I need to heal. I was not ready for her to leave me.

I cannot imagine getting over the bumps in the road without her. I will set my heart at the memories of the life we shared as I find the time I need. If only everyone around me could stop and hear my sobs of sorrow. To recognize that I feel I am alone! I am hurting! I know this is not possible because life does go on, my pain will lessen, and I shall laugh again.

I have searched for comfort in the written word by reading all the books dealing with the loss of a loved one. I find no comfort in them. I don't know if there is even anyone to comfort me. I feel alone because I am alone. I hide the pain so well. I do not know how to ask for help. How sad that those who do know me are not capable of seeing the pain in my eyes. I am no longer a child but a woman who shows and gives love willingly, yet there is no one here for me. I feel as if everyone has forgotten her in just four months' time. Even though I have this great void in my life since she went away, I can still find comfort that she was proud of me and that what we shared was exceptional.

Time does heal all as they say. I have laughed again. I have found my peace. I have moved forward. It has been five years since I began to write about the pain I felt by my mom's death. I have learned to feel compassion and love towards death. I was not the first to lose a loved one, but I felt like I was the only person in the world to have lost a mom. Death strikes us all. Death hurts like no other pain can. Those who do not understand this pain have not lost. At first it hurt so much it was as if I was having my heart torn apart. I had felt pain deeply for the untimely death of my brother and nephew, but not like this. To finally be able to comprehend that life is eternal and only the body is no more has helped me tremendously.

I look back on these past years and realize it is the pain of not having a mom any longer that saddens me the most. It does not matter if she was a sane mom or an insane mom. What matters is that she is no longer. The connection is broken. The emptiness will be forever. I cannot feel this pain any longer though. It has floated off into space. Is my life any different now or less overwhelming? I would have to say that basically I am just older without a mother.

I looked up the word death and read that it was the act of dying; the end of life; the total and permanent cessation of all the vital functions of an animal or plant. I see that even in the dictionary we are considered an animal that once was living and breathing but now ceases to exist. The important blinking word for me was "permanent." How true this feeling of death is. Something we cannot control or bring back. We cannot erase death by saying "we're sorry" – can we?

I then proceeded to look up the word pain and to learn that one of its meanings is mental or emotional suffering or torment. This is a pain that one cannot put a bandage on or take a pill to heal. The only remedy would be time. To try and walk someone through this pain cannot be done by another. One must walk along this path alone. It is true I have learned that time does heal all. The memories of a life can never be truly forgotten. To love no matter what and fill with pain is part of living. The unknown is what frightens us. The promise of tomorrow and seeing a loved one again we choose not to believe.

Compassion is a feeling of deep sympathy and sorrow for another's suffering or misfortune accompanied by a desire to alleviate the pain or remove its cause. I wonder and ask myself, how could there be so many people today who lack compassion for those they supposedly love? We are all guilty of living for today and making ourselves the main priority in life. I learned through the many years of illness and Gracie's struggles to be compassionate. I chose many occasions to share my time, to give of myself, to listen, and to hear when others spoke of their own fears. I accepted those in need as well as my mom into my life as they are. I may not agree all of the time and wonder why people say and do what they do but I accept people as they are. I loved her. No questions asked.

I agree I was in deep pain and hurting at the loss and trauma of dealing with my mom's cancer and then death but I learned so much from her. Isn't that what life's experiences are about – to learn and change for the better? How do we all forget that death is permanent? We are a society of people that haggle over the little problems of life that disgust us. When in reality the picture is so much bigger than we care to see. It all comes down to the feeling of pain, which we do not know what to do with because we are afraid of feeling.

When I started writing I was sad and hurting and feeling sorry for myself. The pain was suffocating me. How selfish of me to dwell on my loss, my pain. I did hurt and then I felt better eventually. All I needed to do was remember that we loved one another unconditionally. Gracie always said that I was the cat's meow, and I simply accepted her as she was for as long as I can remember.

Death, Pain, and Compassion – three words that say it all! Death as permanent as life is not! Pain as hurtful as one can imagine! Compassion for those who are dying, dead, or living! We can try and help those in pain by simply being aware. I have been witness to so many of us who are not aware of our own actions or the actions of others. To love is to hurt. For we choose to exist in life not accepting a daily existence that God chooses for us. When we admit to this fact, we can become aware and fill with love.

I am capable of saying proudly that I am not afraid to show love for another, to feel compassion for those who are struggling today. I learned that death brings pain and is part of our existence. Time is what moves us forward from death and eases the pain for some. There are many people who never get over the loss of a loved one and stay filled with sorrow for what was and what will never be. I want answers to life, death, and eternity.

It seems to me as I journal daily that it is the best time for me to hear the voice of my soul. I find comfort and guidance in the words that I write. I truly believe that the spoken word is a clue to all that one must express to find one's truth. I know that my life as Gracie's daughter has ended, but as that door is closing another is beginning to open.

I travelled along with Gracie during the last thirty years of her path through the halls of many hospitals with locked doors, unbelievable abuse, and cries during the day, as well as the night, from those who were forgotten. Many people that I met were also classified as living in the world of the insane. Gracie had many acquaintances in these places but no true friends or visits from anyone but me as I look back on yesterday.

There is so much I crave to know, to learn, to experience on this journey at this time in my life. As a woman in her midlife years I am amazed at how excited I feel as I search for myself and knowledge. I have many questions that I need answers to, but my main question is: why was Gracie considered insane?

Chapter Two

Searching

Amanda began searching and looking for answers. Her belief that the road of life can either break or mend a person filled her daily with questions. Her whole life poured from her fingers now onto the pages of her journal. A lifetime of memories to sort through that showed her the reasons why she struggled today with the loss of Gracie. In her writings she became witness to many lessons in life that she had learned. She liked to say that she was soul searching. She would sit and dream and search her mind for answers until she found the peace to set her free of the nightmares of yesterday.

At the top of the page the first words she wrote startled her as she began… Loneliness fills my soul. I can dig deep into myself and remember the little girl and smile at who I had been. Unfortunately, the little girl does not smile back. She is scared and lost. Sorrow has crawled into her life throughout the years and darkness is with her always now. She has this feeling that there is fear and pain and more heartbreak waiting for her down the road.

The first years of yesterday play back like a movie in my mind in stages. I was little, starting kindergarten, making my First Holy Communion, dressed all in white like a bride. I would look into the mirror and see my face look back at me: a happy glow in my eyes. I believed in God and was a good girl. My heart filled with love as a child for all. Years would pass and then I had my Confirmation and Sweet Sixteen. I grew up in the generation that always did as it was told by their parents. Never disobey or be disrespectful or lie or cheat another. Just a few years past my sixteenth birthday I would marry and become a wife. I went from becoming a good daughter to a good wife. Stepping one foot in front of the other on my road of life I would next become a good mother. Silently and quickly I erased the little girl, yet I craved to be her still.

I had a ball being a mom, almost as much fun as being that little girl. The only time I stayed true to her was as a mom. I played and filled with love for the children I created. I rejoiced in being a mom. I encouraged, loved, and supported them entirely. I fell into motherhood as if I had been programmed to be just that – a mom! My love for my children is beyond what one would term unconditional. I dedicated myself to them and respected them as unique individuals. I am not saying that I was a friend to them but in the end I have become their friend. I have always treated them as people with minds and wishes and dreams that can come true for them.

I have always tried to explain people and life to them as a parent. I was able to give them options and for them to see the other way, for there can always be another way. I am a lot older but at times they are a lot wiser. I was capable of teaching and learning from them, as well as being their mother. At times I worry: can I love them so much or too much? I enforce in them the strength to be true to themselves, to stand tall and proud of their accomplishments. Like every mother, my wish for my children is that they remember these beliefs I have taught them and for them to live loving, productive, happy lives.

The vicious cycle of teaching handed down from the parent to the child I believe can be the opposite of one's own upbringing to an extent, at least in my case. At times I question if I am living through the eyes of my children. Trying to create a life for them that can be better than the one I grew up in. Can this even be possible when already they have so much more than I ever had? My life growing up was much simpler than the child of today. That in itself tells me that I have accomplished all that I can for them.

The gift of children goes beyond diapers, cooking, homework, and teaching. For me it has been a lifetime of companionship, joy, and a unit of love that I get to be a part of daily. My pride in these people that I gave birth to fills my heart with overflowing wonderment, love, and respect. The greatest part of my existence has been my children. They add to my life a light that burns brightly.

I am at a crossroads today only because I have set out to find peace and love from within for myself. The need to learn the lesson of forgiveness towards people that I feel abused by through the passing of time. I can remember the day my mom tried to end her own life. The sadness and pain that I felt for this woman at this difficult time that she had to try to commit suicide. How did no one see she was hurting? We are all guilty of saying we love, but do we really? The agony that my mother was not mentally ill filled me for years. The hardest part of her illness was that I saw a different person surface in my own father. I did not like what I saw and I did not understand when he walked away from her. In one single action on their path in life they changed mine. I found an inner strength to love this woman and I am so thankful to God that I was granted the privilege to be her daughter. For my entire life I showered her with unconditional love that goes beyond a parent and a child or even a husband and a wife. I believed that she was my responsibility and cared for her as I did my own children.

The years seemed to fly by filled with diapers, babies, and my mom Gracie needing me. Sometimes she was institutionalized and sometimes she was actually sane it seemed to me. I always feared the unknown only because of what she tried at one time to do. I begged her to live with us but she refused because it was not her place to do so. She believed like all people believe that society has the power to label us and place us in a place they choose for those who are different. She coveted her world of the mentally ill and found a need to live in it.

I found it extremely interesting for people to joke that she was "crazy" – ha – ha – ha! I could feel the little girl inside of me cringe but the smile on my face told everyone differently. The little girl loved her totally, as her mom. She was more a lost soul, misplaced, and I believed she just needed acceptance and love from someone. I incorporated her as best I could into the lives of my family and gave her the love she searched for. My role as a good wife was simple. I never was one to ask questions and knew very well how to hide my sorrow. If anyone were to meet me they would never be able to tell the battles I fought on a daily basis in my own mind. I accepted, growing up in that other generation, that my husband was the boss and that I was to listen to him. I chalked it up to the fact that he had a stronger personality than I. His needs were different than mine, and I felt sad that he was not capable of kindness. I accepted him and loved him. I remembered the screaming and fighting between my own parents and refused to do likewise. I wondered at times if all men believed they needed to act mean. I honestly can say now at this age that as I look back on my life, the little girl never was one to make waves. She grew up into a woman who also did not have the desire to stand up for what she wanted. It was always easier to agree or to not care. Being confrontational was not part of who I was or who I am even today. All my life my wants did not matter as much; I convinced myself of this belief. I have to admit that there were times where I actually did not even care and it was so much easier to go along with what my parents and husband were demanding of me. Like the little girl, the woman I became learned to know her place and do what was expected of her.

As a mom I was able to have more fun. I was able to play with live dolls, to dress them up and enjoy myself tremendously. I cooked, cleaned, loved them, and laughed with them daily. I was so involved in being a mom and wife that I created a world where the outside did not exist. I neither wanted nor needed anything from anyone. I was complete and happy in my life. As a little girl I was proud to be, and as a mom and wife I was proud to do. I was happy being good.

Suddenly, without warning my brother would be dead. This was the first death in my life that crushed my heart. I was angry, mad, confused, and very, very sad that he was gone. I searched for reasons why until I became aware that it simply was his time to die. Death is part of life and we have no control over it. Then without warning my nephew would be taken. An unnecessary and untimely death, it would make me appreciate how precious life truly is and to acknowledge this. As a wife and mother my greatest fear has always been the loss of one of my own. Here I was witness to those I loved dying and there was nothing I could do about it. This was a new kind of fear that started to seep in and fill my every thought. The fear of death of one of my own would crush me totally.

Now that my mom has also died, I am at a loss for words when it comes to her. Here was a woman that was truly a part of my life. I saw her weekly and in the last year of her life almost daily. When she was diagnosed with lung cancer I cried. I knew her end would come. In the last two weeks of her life, I held her hand, I wiped her brow, I kissed her forehead, and I gave her ice chips to cool her dry cracked lips. I waited for the end to come, yet I found I was still not ready when she drew her last breath. Even today I am not ready for her to not be a part of my life. I will always miss her. I saw her still and silent with peace on her face in the glow of a dimly lit room but in my heart I feel she is waiting for my weekly visit still. It hurts too much to believe that she has left me.

It was such a long time ago when I first lost my mom to the world of mental illness that it became acceptable that she would live this way forever. Then after the death of my brother and nephew, I imagined she would also outlive me. I became even closer to her in the last year of her life. It seemed to me that she might just be sane after all. It began to make me question if she was ever insane. When she was told she was manic-depressive my world crumbled. However, like everything I do, I never questioned it. I simply accepted what I was told. Is this a blessing in disguise for me? I wondered. Now I ask myself if she could have lived a productive life out of the institutions. Should I have checked her out with other doctors? These thoughts fill my head all because a sane mother resurfaced from my childhood in the end. I fear today that I could have made a difference in her life and didn't. It makes me want to find out about this road we all travel down. Was there a detour I could have taken as her daughter? At an early age in her own life she walked away from so much and never looked back. Like her I am capable of an unquestionable acceptance of life which is a unique trust I see today that many lack.

Throughout all of the years, I could talk to her about anything and she would help me in her own way. How does someone replace this loss? How could she possibly be considered insane by society when she comforted and loved me? I love my children and I fear for them when they realize how this love can hurt. The greatest fear I possess is that the time will come one day when I shall be out of control. I too can become ill and not be able to help myself. I try my best to keep it together, but what if one day I cannot? In all the books I have read everything is hereditary. The genes carry from generation to generation: the good and the bad, the healthy and the sick.

I tend to grow stronger through my writing, for the release in my head helps me to ease the pain. When I write it is almost like a cleansing of my soul. I feel the need to tell my story to continue on. This communication to paper helps me to understand myself. I do wonder where the little girl has gone. Every now and then I see the resemblance of her in my daily routine. She lies within and I hold her tender to my heart for she is the best part of me. However, the road took a turn and left me here where I am now.

Each one of us is given a road to travel. There are bridges to cross and many forks lie ahead in the road. We make our own choices but then can these same choices be called our destiny? In the circle of family, friends, and acquaintances our roads become intertwined with one another. We can laugh and cry together but only the one in pain can help oneself. I accepted the pain I have felt throughout my life for I am learning from this pain. I will feel sadness at even the loss of my pain as I grow.

Our destiny is in the stars and whichever one we follow leads down the road of life that waits at the end of tomorrow. No one knows what tomorrow will bring. I have decided to gather my strength from these words my mom said when she found out she had cancer. One day at the doctor's she looked at me as she sat on the table waiting to be examined and said, "I have lived a good life." In disbelief, I wondered to myself how she can even think this. Who am I to judge her if this is what she believed? I thought about her words and knew the life she lived and realized she accepted her life through these years as it was. She did not question her illness, or need answers to her life. I never heard her say or ask, "Why me?" So in answer to all of my questions I must remember the beliefs of my mom and the words she spoke to me that day. When I take a look at my life and if the road I am traveling comes to an end tomorrow, I know today that I have lived a good life.

I have been journaling and writing forever. I have learned that poetry, something that comes to me very easily, is a comfort. As I begin to share my life with you, the reader, I wish that you will understand how easy it was for me to become a believer. I traveled the road of my life and all that has come to me on this path brought me where I am today.

In doing all I have done with the belief that I could do it with love as my mantra, I was capable of asking nothing of anyone. It was not a priority in my life. I accepted those I loved as the people they chose to be. I enjoyed doing for others. This is my silent strength.

Chapter Three

Belief

Amanda thought to herself that the emptiness in her heart at the loss of Gracie was really about what? She herself struggled with her own beliefs through the years. Always she followed her gut feelings and her intuition. She could never find herself capable of hurting another with words or actions. It troubled her to the point of silence. Today she questioned what she wanted for her own daughters. Through the years she tried to do all with love as her foundation and belief. The void in her life was great without Gracie and she wondered today if her choices in life and how she lived had been enough for those she loved. Abuse both verbal and mental had been part of her existence forever. Having been told in the past that she was a person who doesn't do anything was the seed that began to grow and start to trouble her. At this age of her life she was herself believing the words of others. She was thinking too much about Gracie. Life had simply been stepping one foot in front of the other for her and she accepted everyone without question. She felt that maybe her silence through life and this attitude started in her childhood. She looked for her journal and knew the words would pour from her soul to tell her the answers.

She started to write and fulfill Gracie's belief that she was indeed an author. My memories of growing up are happy and simple. I can recall being lonely as a child. I remember an imaginary friend. I was a very content child and listened to my parents. I was asked to help my mother with dinner and cleaning the house. I felt love but yet there was a detachment. At times I felt as a child that I was responsible for my mother and her happiness. If I listened and kept her calm all would be well. An inner need was planted to grow that I craved to have someone take care of me even at a young age. No one in my entire life has ever asked me what I wanted or needed. I never thought that I was too young or inexperienced to take care of others. For years I never dreamed of being anything else except a wife and mother. My generation catered to their men and took care of the house. During troubled times with my mother even my father turned to me to care for her. I became the strength in our family. I existed by helping those who were weaker than I. As a child I never questioned my parents or the type of home life I lived. This type of existence has now come full circle. I have lived a life in this world as being one who does as she is told.

I believed as a child, as a teen, and as a woman that everything I have done in my life was because I did it with love. A love that to me has always been unconditional, no questions asked. I put all before me. Now it seems through the passing of these years I erased my own identity. I lived my life caring for an ill mom, raised my children to be the unique individuals God has destined them to be, and stood by my husband's side, no questions asked. All these years a pattern has been set for them all to witness. Today I see a change in myself starting to form. The role I played has come to its end. A new role awaits me and has been ignited by an inner dream of mine to accomplish my own creation. I can even look at this time as a chance for a new life, or a renewal of who I believe I am meant to be. Yet, it is part of my life. I have stayed true to my childhood belief of reading and writing. Today this is a comfort and strength for me to read my own words. In doing so, I will create and follow this path that I am now capable of walking.

My children have strength and power to be individuals. I have always supported them to be the people they need to be. They all have beauty and talent of their own. They are capable of love, understanding, and acceptance. All I pray for now is that they create satisfying existences and live a lifetime that is fulfilling and creative for them.

The chores of my life have now ended and I am proud that I never pushed my children to endure for me. I always believed it was my job as a wife and a mother to fulfill the responsibility of my role by creating a home that would be a safe haven for all. Through this belief I have been able to encourage my children to do their own thing. Times are different now and I appreciate that my daughters have a say in this world. I as their mother raised them to believe this. With my support and encouragement they have the chance to make choices and follow their dreams.

What I chose to do with my life was the choice to dismiss my wants and desires to care for those I loved. To do it with love was my remedy for happiness while doing all that I did. No one ever understood that I had set priorities and I enjoyed my life. I am happy and have always been as a housewife and mother for all these years. I was never given options and I accepted this. My husband gave me the greatest life because I was allowed to do what I was good at. I knew how to be a good wife and a great mother. The lesson of unconditional love is in reality to learn the lesson of acceptance for those we love. No judgment, no criticism, no anger, no hate – just acceptance. I set them up as being the most important experience in my life to learn from. In doing so, I am now ready to move forward for I have learned many lessons from yesterday.

I need now to create for myself. I have a desire burning in my chest to be successful and help those in need. My children are grown and their need of me is less. I have the time to do something that I am passionate about. My choice is to tell a story about unconditional love, acceptance, compassion, respect, honesty, trust, peace, and belief. All I know is that I write in my mind when I cook, when I walk, when I lie in bed at night, even while watching television I am writing. To be published will be a dream come true. In reality, it has always been mine, as well as Gracie's.

This miracle of a life I have shared with my children was an enormous gift from God. I remember the teen years as the time they began to spread their wings. It is when they were getting themselves, as well as me, ready for them to leave. The knowledge that my children have been only a gift to me as their parent resurfaced when they became adults. I see they need me in a different way now. As their mother my life is filled with many tender moments and treasured memories. I placed them in a box in my mind and stored them away until I need the comfort of yesterday. The mind like a camera can call the past forward as if it were a snapshot. I have many fine treasures in my box to pull out now and then. Without even realizing it themselves my children have memories of their own that one day will bring a tear or a smile to their lips. To live a life accomplished in the choices I have made and the love I have given enlightens me today. I have no regrets and no guilt.

I wonder of the values and outcome down the road for my children. The sorrows, pain, and disappointment that life will have in store for each of them at different times are exactly that part of life we all experience and grow from. I know they take with them my love that I have shared every day of their lives with them. As the parent, I believed I was to guide, support, and encourage, not criticizing, condemning, or neglecting the dreams of my children. I respected them as I wished to be respected myself.

I have never regretted the years and hours I shared with them. I do regret the lack of those to not understand my choice. Regret is a strong word to use because I enjoyed my choices and therefore I was good at this life I lived. Today I see that I am now able to move on with an open heart. I am free to be me.

I give credit to the mom who works. How does she do it all? She has two jobs compared to my one and the end result for her is that she is able to accomplish creativity and motherhood. I applaud the working mother of today. I give praise to her strength. I marvel at her ability to believe in herself. To choose such a hard existence – for we all know there is never praise and love from the outside world for the role of motherhood nevertheless the working mom.

Turning fifty a few years after Gracie's death filled me with strangling tears of fear. I amazed myself as I became witness to a fear of life and everything that I had to look forward to. Tears were my constant companion and I did not know how to stop them. I felt that I had traveled halfway, and now what? For the life of me I was unable to see what was expected of me down the road. I had succeeded in going up the ladder of life but now I felt the steps had disappeared and I was sliding downward. In reading my own words and creating a well of knowledge for me to draw from, I rebuilt the steps on my slide and very slowly I shall walk down them. The road lies before me going in many directions. Time is now mine. This road is beckoning me to stand up and make a difference. I shall write and manifest my dream so that maybe, just maybe, if I do it with love my voice will be heard.

My daily journal entries have an inner voice that is screaming to be heard. I have been consumed for years with the jobs of daughter, wife, and mother that no longer need my entire support. Gracie has moved on to her home in heaven; my children are living their own lives, and my husband and I share a slower life today. I look at this man today that I have loved all my life and although we are not the same to look at as we were, the love between us is comfortable, secure, filled with tenderness and an invisible bond that allows us to finally be accepting of one another.

Chapter Four

Acknowledge

L ife has changed drastically for me. Slowly now I am crawling out of my shell. Cautiously I am starting to breathe like a free woman. Creatively I am enjoying myself. Daily I am witness to my empty life. I have become aware of the windows of my soul as they gently open. I can see and smell the freshness of my essence. The girl from yesterday is reaching forward trying to make me remember her. I find myself apologizing for burying her so deeply.

Still hiding under the covers I dream of words to make me understand. Another day has begun. I will get up and do what? Look for myself I imagine! In my early fifties how did I get to be afraid of myself? For years I imagined I was in control of my life. Who am I kidding? I have never been in control of my life. I just existed in the life God gave to me by being accepting of all that is in my life.

During this life I lived, I wrote whenever I was troubled or filled with pain. Another gift from God to help me heal myself, I imagine today, as I look back on words that spilled from my soul. My writings seem to be a collection of words that I can look back on and wonder how I let the spirit of my life be drained from me so easily. I buried myself alive to be able to care for others. By putting them first I had no other choice but to silence myself.

As a young girl I was happy, felt loved, and believed I was to do great things. All little girls must feel this way I imagine. In accepting to erase myself in the past, today I believe that was essential for me to experience and learn all that was necessary to take me to where I am today at this very moment. I can recall and imagine the giggling girl that was happy so long ago, even today. I look around at other women that I know, and that I see on the street, wondering if they erased the girl from yesterday too. And, if so, why did they choose like me to become someone else? I crave and need to know these answers. I am searching for how I willingly became silent. Is it easier than to fight? To agree and not make waves must have been easier for me than to be heard and live wholly as a person, to in time become wallpaper, a backdrop to my own life.

The little girl I am talking about was a good Catholic girl with the desire like all good Catholic girls to be a nun. The nuns made me their pet. Like a pet I was patted on the head when I did well. Is that when the desire to be good cultivated itself? To be praised, accepted, and acknowledged that I was good and special. Brought up to believe my parents were next in line to God. Their word was sacred. I had to listen, be honest, and loving at all times.

My husband who became like my parents next in line to be the person I must obey. A strong man with the belief he needed to control his entire family. Obey-obey-obey or you get punished. We were married very young and only had that which our own parents taught us to take into our marriage. I had a weak mother as did he with strong, stubborn powerful fathers that ruled the roost. We learned very well from those who raised us.

Every day now I am searching for answers. I think and think of the personalities I have lived with and allowed to blossom. Yet, daily, weekly, monthly, yearly, I became more and more silent. I allowed myself to become invisible so that they would thrive. Today I believe this is the only acceptable answer for me to acknowledge.

I ask myself at this time in my life if I have empty-nest syndrome or just experiencing a midlife crisis. Am I crazy like my mom? I am wondering if it is my destiny today, or tomorrow, to go crazy too. Then another question arises from the depths of my mind, "What makes someone go crazy?"

A pattern has formed in my life. My silence has enabled those I love to be heard. In supporting them and their beliefs they feel they are wiser than I will ever be. I do not know if I appear weak to them or just not knowing of life because I live in a cocoon so to speak. Yes, I believe in helping them find their way and through their lives I was able to silence my desires to encourage theirs. Lately though I forget to remain silent. That doesn't sound right to me. I don't want to be silent anymore. I believe I too have the right to speak. I learn things and a feeling gets stirred up inside that fills me with excitement and wonder. I want and need to share my knowledge. My cocoon is cracking open and a new world is opening for me to learn from. They do not know who I am now that I have desires and needs. Time has come for change and I see how programmed we all can become. I only want to be a better me.

Unfortunately, for all of them that I love they do not read. They laugh at me and tease me saying that I could just sit in a corner with a book and stay quietly there forever. That would be boring I say to myself. Is that what they really think I am about? That I would sit in a corner and read and not be part of life? Yes, I love to read. I crave the knowledge I find within my precious books. Even as a young child books were my best friend. But, I do not want to be placed in a corner and just read. I am guilty of dreaming and in dreaming I am able to escape into the written word.

I have always wondered if my mom had any inclination that she would be labeled one day as a manic-depressive and live the rest of her life in and out of institutions until the day she died, considered "crazy."

Are we able to even feel if we are going crazy? How do our lives change so drastically? What really happens to the person we were?

I ask myself at times if I know anything. Do I have any tastes of my own to speak of? A favorite word of my husband's when speaking of me is to say I am plain. A word that I feel does not describe me at all. My tastes are less extravagant than his. I like simple things – beautiful, meaningful objects surrounding me. Of course as I have written I love books, flowing curtains in the breeze, candlelight, sitting in the sun letting the rays warm me, reading, and dreaming of writing a bestseller. I have a desire to walk on the beach for years now with the waves crashing before my eyes and just taking in the beauty of nature. Then I wonder, is this enough to complete me and for me to live a meaningful enough life to believe in myself? These are the questions that float in my mind. This is what has become of me after a lifetime of loving, caring, nurturing, and becoming the person they all needed. Am I the only woman who feels this way? Will I just get up one morning and get taken away to a hospital, injected with drugs, and visited on Sunday from then on? Maybe they won't even visit. Could they all feel that because my mom was labeled crazy that I too will end up crazy? Is this the mentality of life?

When I was a child the saying was sticks and stones can break my bones but words can never harm me. If ever I were asked if there were words that I heard that lied to me when I was a child, I would have to recite these. How foolish of the person to say such a rhyme. Bruises fade and pain subsides but words linger on in the mind. Mean, frightened faces are forever burned in my mind of the people who have abused me with ugly comments.

"Shut up, you're nobody and you'll never be anybody, you're not educated enough to be a writer, you have a pretty face but why don't you lose weight, shut up, I've waited my whole life for you to get skinny, you eat so little why are you fat, don't tell anyone you work out with a trainer – they won't believe you, my sister had four kids but she took care of her body right afterwards, don't you wish you were still young and looked like the girls we saw tonight, don't you ever look in the mirror, are you going out dressed like that, do you have makeup on, you're crazy like your mother, shut up, what do you know, nobody likes you, you're sick in the head, something is wrong with you, you have no taste, you're plain, you're an idiot!" These are some of the words that have never harmed me, as the rhyme says! I became a silent woman because of these words. I could not understand saying such words to anyone. A bit confused I would absorb these words into my psyche and imagine what possesses a person who loves me to speak to me in this manner?

I have learned that people speak without thinking. My husband would deny any of the above comments that he has spat out at me. I always wanted to tape his lovely words but I never knew the precise moment of his attack. Of course, these are not only his words but also people I have shared my life with, just like he is not the only husband who is critical of their wife. I know of others but the sad part is that they are not aware of the pain these words cause. I had the strength to silence myself and the ability to not believe today finally any of these comments. I worry about the wives, daughters, and other women who are constantly abused by the people they love.

Doesn't it all come down to being nice to one another? To truly loving each other as we are. I just need to understand how a lovely, lively, full of adventure, fun to be with, easygoing, so much to talk about, happy in love young girl turned into silent me. I look into the mirror and see that young girl inside holding on by the tips of her fingers begging to be pulled out. She craves to join the world and laugh again.

I believe that a long time ago I accepted I was less important than others in my life. In my own mind I became beneath them so to speak, which enabled them to thrive. It was a choice I made that suited me then. The choices I made yesterday do not work today and so I am learning to know the depths of my own heart and who I am and where I am meant to go. I know that I am not the only woman

31

out there that feels this way only because I see sadness in the eyes of many and behind this sadness is their secret of abuse.

Once I started to soul search, as I like to call it, wow, I dug up some heavy memories. I am a good person but at times weak. My husband – a loving, good man – is extremely strong and controlling. My children know they are loved and what is right and wrong. Life came upon me in a manner that I accepted. I showed my husband that he was the boss that he controlled me and I was just a housewife. To let him abuse me with words was maybe a mistake but it allowed me to listen and hear. This I believe to be a unique gift of mine. When he would speak critical or nasty to me I heard him in reality telling me how he was filled with fear and pain. He was not accepting of his own life. In my head I was able to escape to a quick Hail Mary while he raved about incidentals that he gave power to over himself. I allowed him power over me because I needed to learn from him acceptance and this is what I am learning about today.

As a child I escaped to the world of books when my parents argued. I married young and my married life was not that different except that my husband was the one yelling at me. I fell victim to the belief of that time that woman was put on earth to obey man. It is amazing to me that in this time and age that I can write such a sentence. Look around at yourself as you read this – how close are you to being a person like me? As my life flashes before my mind now it is amazing the thoughts that pop into my head when I lie in bed or brush my teeth or drive in my car. A quick flash of yesterday reminds me of a life that today feels to me like it belonged to someone else.

The greatest part about my entire life has been my joy in books, their smell, their look, and the words inside from cover to cover. This love of reading began when I was a little girl and survived even until today. I need to have books around me to survive. This is good. This is a sign of the little girl I was. Something I was never able to erase. My love for the written word was too strong to eliminate.

I look back and realize today that I have always been true to myself and never was mean to another. I miss my mom and relish in the fact that I was a great daughter. I question that maybe I shouldn't have changed and become weak in the eyes of my children and husband. Yet I needed to survive too in life and be able to nurture and love. In all honesty I now am witness to an inner guidance that I was given to silence myself during a time I needed to do the job I undertook. As a wife and a parent I believed in what I succumbed to and agreed upon as my role. My truth is that there is a reason for everything and a purpose.

A sweet calmness has come over me the last few months, like a crisp breeze from the ocean while walking on the beach. I am at peace. I looked for something I had lost. I succeeded in finding a memory from yesterday. Actually, the girl that I had believed was erased is now a woman of today who is filled with knowledge and understanding of yesterday. I see life from the eyes of a woman in her fifties but inside the glow of youth shines brightly. I am happy. I wrote my words through the years as if they were open wounds from a beating. I have recovered from the past and I am about to move forward. Are you curious as to what I have learned? My answer is to tell you to love, to be kind, to support your family, to do little things that matter to you as a person. I wrote, I read, I played with my children, and I listened to my children, as I prepared their home and a life filled with their own memories. If I made mistakes I'm sure I'll be forgiven. We need to learn that there is no right or wrong way to experience life except to live it truthfully which is the lesson to grow from. Life is filled with ups and downs, love and hate, sadness and gladness, fun times and favorite memories. I have all of mine! Dig deep inside and find yours.

I marvel at the peace I have found. I am no different than any other woman in the world. We forget our dreams to make the dreams of our children come true. We erase our needs to support the needs of the man we love. We become the companion to those who need us as we acquire a silent strength from within to guide us. Being a wife and a mother is the most difficult job we will ever encounter. The pay the best we'll ever receive. I can recall small hands in mine or wrapped around my neck as I was hugged tightly. In the photo gallery of life I have images of babies suckling at my breast. The many achievements in their own lives fulfilled mine proudly. No amount of money can ever erase the faces of joy, love, and happiness I have stored away. The crazy times, the arguments, and difficult child-rearing years are looked back on now as I chuckle at the loving memories.

Inside the inner glow of light from sheer love and happiness lights up my face daily as I look in the mirror. People comment that I look younger and different. I have a secret. I am at peace.

I started looking for the girl from yesterday and she surfaced on her own, full of goodness and love. I feel her inside me. I remember her needs, wants, and desires. I am amazed that she waited for me. Now we embrace one another as we walk off into the world of acceptance.

Right now you are wondering, what about her husband? Well, I love and believe in him. I'll be the first to agree he does not know how to speak, but guess what – he makes me laugh. He has taught me patience, respect, acceptance, and tolerance. We are parents and created a lifetime together. We have substance to us. Memories, some happy, others sad, but life is just that; sometimes happy – sometimes sad. As a little girl I was never a quitter and I always believed in the good of people. The bottom line: my husband is a good man. He and I are maturing together and I feel a quiet, in-the-background kind of love from him. He is trying to understand me as I grow and spread my wings. This is the difference in our relationship today compared to yesterday. He did not know any better than I how to act. We are all capable as we grow to be the parents we can be, not to follow the parent who raised us in any kind of pain. Children learn from what they see and experience. Only the strong filled with love and beliefs are capable to change for the better. Once I explained to him that he was making me feel abused by his choice of words, he made a complete U-turn and now tries to correct the words that come out of his mouth. He is willing to try and change. How many men out there will not even try?

I feel I am lucky because the girl from yesterday never quit or better yet never had the guts to leave. In the end I have dug deep inside myself and filled my eyes now with her bright essence. I am filled with love for myself.

Amanda gathered her journals and looked at the collection of words she has accumulated since the death of Gracie. Suddenly she remembers as if waking from a trance Gracie's writings. Her mother's words fill her with emotion: "Save All My Writings, A Book Is In The Making Through My Daughter!" The time had finally come for her to tell the story of Gracie's escape to the mansions in her mind.

- Chapter Five -

Escape

Amanda started from the beginning, from the Gracie of years ago. Recalling their conversations and the feelings that she was witness to in Gracie, she began with trembling fingers to write the story of her mother's escape from the world. In her mind's image she saw Gracie as she had so many times throughout the years in her room. She stifled her emotions and knew the process of writing from her heart about Gracie would make the difference in her portrayal of her mother. She closed her eyes for a moment, took a deep breath, as she began to see Gracie in the mirror of her mind and to dig deep into the mansions of Gracie's mind which she had come to know and respect. She began to write!

Gracie searched in her pocket for her sunglasses. When she found them she placed them on her face. Gracie believed the eyes were the windows of the soul. If she covered them she felt safe. She began to make her way down the sterile pale-green hallway with its black and white checkerboard floor. Looking into the rooms as she went by she imagined that she lived in a college dormitory, as she touched the sunglasses on her face. Each room had only a bed with a chair and a dresser. Until one chose to look closely then and only then would they notice also that there was no display of a personality, no pictures, no resemblance of any type of connection to a family! No special display was visible that these people belonged possibly anywhere else in this world.

As she dragged her feet towards her room she looked into the empty eyes of the other people she lived with as she passed them in the hall. Everyone looked the same, vacant eyes, sad and scary looking to others. One face, one attitude! Don't bother me and I won't bother you. Sometimes, a youngster under fifty years old would be admitted. At first anxious to have a friend, but then medication would void out the need for any wants or desires. Medication had just been given now and it was time to rest. One by one they all came to a halt, to a nonhuman robotic form. She laughed to herself. She had been resting for the past twenty years.

Quietly, Gracie lay on the bed as tears rolled down her face; a sweet calmness filled her insides. The after effect of the medication always left her mellow. If she stayed perfectly still breathing in and out she would simply drift off. Images of another life, a younger Gracie, a family would float around in her mind. She could almost see herself in her kitchen preparing dinner for her husband. His favorite meal had always been the American diet: steak, potatoes, vegetables, and salad. He had been her life and reason for living. She tried now to smell the coffee as it perked for their after-dinner dessert.

Her eyes began to flutter in anticipation of opening. She tried to stay calm. She did not want to open her eyes yet, for Gracie knew when she opened them reality would slap her across the face. Almost brutally she would feel beaten. Confused! Anxious! Doubting her whereabouts! The sterile room would begin to focus in. There was a narrow bed with its rough coarse sheets, the thin worn-out old blanket, and flat pillow. Once her eyes opened she could see the peeling paint above her head on the ceiling. She would begin to hear voices from the hallway and realize she was living behind locked doors. She was institutionalized. Then she would think to herself that she was safe; her medication and food were given to her three times a day, and even the clothes she wore were not her own. She always wondered though where her clothes were and whose clothes she was wearing. Her biggest concern was what had happened to that woman whose clothes she was given to wear and why her feet were so big. This was her reality.

That was the reason she liked to escape to what she referred to as the mansions of her mind. Never did she let anyone into this secret place. Especially the doctors who were not aware of these escapes into her mind. For Gracie that was her sole enjoyment – the only thing that was truly hers – no one could control her mind but her. Her imagination was wild as she traveled to these mansions.

He was tall, with dark wavy hair that smelled clean like soap and fresh always. He was very handsome with movie-star looks – a dream come true, as they said. His body was muscular but not bulky, skin soft but not mushy. She loved his dark hair the best. Everyone remarked at the resemblance to one another they shared. She was almost the same height at 5'8" and dark like him but thinner with legs that went on and on, he always reminded her of this asset. Her greatest feature was her green eyes combined with her own black shiny hair and white porcelain skin. She was a real knockout, he would tell her. Actually, she felt always too tall for a girl – no one could ever call her a petite little thing. She stood with her back straight, her chest out, and held her head high whenever she walked by his side. Proud that he had chosen her. Feeling special for the love he gave to her. At times wondering and being afraid that he had made a mistake. How could she be so lucky to be loved by this man?

In her heart now she felt her love for him was her way of believing he was still part of her world. They had shared their dreams and made their promises for life. She felt the tears sting her eyes. Like always they slowly slipped down her face and wet her cheeks. He had betrayed her. He had broken her heart. He was gone from her life.

Whenever he had made love to her she could smell his cologne on her body afterwards. Excitement filled every corner of her inner being at the thought of him. He taught her so well how to make her body respond to his slightest touch. He had promised to fill her entire life with love and happiness. He had vowed to love her until death do us part. Words – words – words swirled around her mind that now meant nothing to her.

As she rested now and dreamed of what had been she could almost hear his voice. She chuckled, as she lay very still with her eyes closed, behind her dark sunglasses picturing the past. A friend of her cousins, he was coming by to borrow her car. Gracie felt the pull in the middle of her stomach, the warm feeling just at the thought of their first meeting. When she opened the door and found herself witness to the beauty of his face she knew he was the one. In all honesty later on they both admitted love at first sight. From that very first meeting they were inseparable. For her it was the beginning of her life.

During this past year over and over she traveled back to these memories it seemed more than ever. She believed in her soul that she didn't want to continue living without him. They were no longer two people but to her through the years had become one. These were the memories that calmed her and soothed her sorrow, and at times made her cry. Gracie felt a chill as she opened her eyes, startled that once again she had escaped only to be forced to return to the truth. Yes, she could feel the coarse blanket in the palm of her hand just as she knew to the right of her was the old chair and dresser. Glancing up, the paint was still peeling. The small dirty window was locked shut with bars. She could almost see the sky through the dirt on a sunny day.

At this time of day it was hard to focus, or was it just the sad, scary feeling as she returned to this world? Gracie believed she belonged in this silent, sad, drugged world she lived in. She accepted it as her life. The rhythm of this place kept her functioning. Her memories kept her alive. The empty feelings inside her were caused by the medication. It erased the Gracie from long ago. In its place was a shell of someone who had a life, and who had lived, as well as once belonged in the big real world. She now wore the label society had given her. At times it felt like it was carved into her forehead. One word said it all: "CRAZY!" Should she believe the doctors when they told her she was mentally ill? Could anyone blame her for trying to end her life? Did anybody care what he had done to her and the pain and disbelief she felt at the love he took away from her? For years her love, her life, her entire purpose on earth was dedicated to him.

Through the years growing up her life was full of freedom that she paid a price for: no one to love her, no one to come home from school to. Maybe it was because her own mother abandoned her when she was very young. In Gracie's mind she saw the little girl she had been, sitting on the front stoop. It was a warm sunny day and she could feel the sun was shining on her face. Boys were playing stickball in the street while girls were jumping rope as she and her friends played on the stoop with their dolls. Her mom was all dressed up and smelled like flowers. She told Gracie to stay outside while she went to the store. Her dad was getting ready for work. She shuddered at this memory, for her mother never returned that day. The little girl from yesterday Gracie could picture in her mind's eye as she felt the cool air suddenly because the sun was no longer in the sky when her dad came towards her. For many years Gracie hated that time of the day when the sun was no longer and the smell of flowers were in the air! That day she was dropped off at her grandparents' house because her father worked nights and she could not stay home alone. Everyone spoke in whispers as they shook their heads when they looked at Gracie. Her cheeks hurt from them all pinching them and patting her head. No one ever told her anything; she just realized that one day she had a mother and then she did not. Her father, a quiet, hard-working man, became extremely silent and withdrawn.

The only time she had with her father was Saturday and Sunday. He called them "Gracie days." He would take her to the park, the movies, or the beach. They would sit for hours watching the water and digging in the sand. He would let Gracie fill up buckets with shells and rocks to take home. Their favorite time of the day was when they bought ice cream on the way back home. When he died of a heart attack Gracie believed what people meant when they said that someone had a broken heart. She began at the age of nine to live with her grandparents. Her father's aunts and uncles were always in and out of her life too, but they had their own families to care about and she basically was handed down clothes and broken toys. She always felt alone, unloved, and unwanted after his death. Only a child herself she became silent and withdrawn for the seed of fear had been planted inside of her to grow.

When Gracie turned sixteen her mom reappeared into her life and insisted she live with her. Still she was not capable of being a mother to her. She had a new boyfriend and was always out dancing. Back then Gracie never realized that her mother was an alcoholic. Yet today she had pictures stored of her in her mind, passed out on the couch, with a drink and an ashtray full of butts. The love Gracie craved from this woman was never given to her. In its place she saw disgust, regret, and anger at the sight of her whenever she looked into her eyes.

Gracie needed a loving relationship and tried to understand why her own mother hated her. At eighteen her mom told her she was an adult now and should act like one. Gracie felt young like a child and lost. She wanted to be hugged and kissed by her mother. Instead her mother left her to fend for herself. They had no relationship to speak of because her mom always did her own thing even when she lived with Gracie.

The day Rob Jewel came into her life and showered her with the long lost kisses and love she craved, Gracie devoured him. She remembered the pain of his betrayal or was it a need she felt in her stomach for a normal family life that she always envisioned. As a child it always seemed too hard to her and so far away to grasp and have. A mom, a dad, a house of her own, and her life would be complete. All of this represented love to her ever since she was a little girl. Finally, he was able as her husband to make her dream come true.

Now at this age living in an institution, why should she remember any of this? Why should she care? In her heart she never discovered the answers to her many questions, for her love for others answered her reason for existence. As Gracie lay on the narrow bed, the feeling of melancholy took over. She placed one foot at a time on the cold linoleum floor checking that her sunglasses were still in place. Her feet were steady but as she looked down she could not remember where her sneakers were. Slowly Gracie paced the room barefoot as memories flooded her mind.

Her life began the day she became Mrs. Rob Jewel. Rob's love engulfed her whole mind. He was her constant. He was what she had dreamed of her whole life. Their vows once taken were their promise to love one another until death. He was all she ever needed or wanted. The power of his love satisfied all her desires and washed away her fears. When the children came they were a complete family unit. She finally felt she belonged somewhere and to someone.

When her son, Rob Jr., was born he stole a piece of her heart away from his father. He was a miniature copy and Gracie's love doubled now for the two men in her life. Not even two years later her daughter, Amanda, was born. Fear would begin to set in, as Gracie believed Amanda stole Rob's love away from her. The battle would begin and Gracie was not happy when Rob bestowed love and gifts on Amanda. Gracie felt the old feelings of loneliness return. The little girl in Gracie's mind would scream, "He belongs to me; he's mine."

She now reached for a cigarette. As she inhaled deeply and felt the smoke float ever so sweetly through her lungs she exhaled into the stark room. Gracie spent most of the day in her room. The aides would check on her because they didn't want her to sleep. You had to be up! She would always yell back at them, "I'm up! – I'm up!" In her mind the words lonely-lonely-lonely screamed.

Her mind began to throb for the memories were always quite painful and difficult even for her to comprehend. For years she relived the past over and over. She was always searching for the reason her world fell apart. Searching for love in her memories, the feeling love provided for her and the security she had felt at one time. She realized today how obsessed with Rob she had become. To her he was even more important than her children. That was how in her mind she rationalized walking away from them so many years ago. It wasn't that there was no love. Her heart ached for them, but she found safety and peace in the mansions of her mind, reliving what to her was the happiest time in her life.

She was unable at one time to control the feelings that sickened her when she saw love in his eyes for Amanda. She believed always he belonged to her. She could remember how the muscles in her face would tighten, bringing her lips up to a sneer. She could never control these feelings. She couldn't explain it to anyone, so she kept it to herself and accepted the doctor's diagnosis that she was a manic-depressive. She herself had to agree for at times she did feel crazy, wild, and out of control.

At one time in their marriage she had lost it and could not control herself. She would walk the streets for hours crazed and wild, talking out loud to herself. Everyone – neighbors, friends, her own children – would see her dirty clothes, dirty hair, and her dirty body. People would stare but keep their distance. Fear she could see on their faces. Fear of the crazy woman! Then for days she would sleep, unable to rise and function in the world as was expected of her.

These past years taking medication helped her to achieve where she needed to go, which was her own mind. She was very content sitting back and letting the world pass her by. Gracie couldn't recall when she slept a full night. The medication had altered her so, that she was amazed at her own reflection in the mirror. Was that what she really looked like? Her beautiful black hair was greasy and gray now, uncut, and needed badly to be brushed. Sometimes she wondered what that smell was and sadly it would dawn on her it was her own body. Her long slender legs were fat and ugly as well as bruised and flabby. Through the years she must have gained over one hundred and fifty pounds. The nicotine from cigarette after cigarette had left her fingers yellow. Her daughter told her that she smoked over three hundred cigarettes a week. She thought to herself, could that be possible? Was it possible to smoke that much and change so drastically?

The hardest part was no teeth. She remembered the day when she actually pulled them right out of her mouth. It was so painful and strange. At first when she discovered her teeth were loose and began to play with them it was a distraction, actually mind-boggling. She herself didn't believe that here she was an adult with her own fingers pulling out her teeth. When she showed her daughter, Amanda was silent and couldn't believe her eyes. She screamed at her, "What are you doing?" Amanda took her to the dentist and he told her she had a severe case of periodontitis, a disease of the gums, which the doctor said is actually the chief cause of loss of teeth after the age of thirty-five. When she accomplished pulling all her teeth out, false teeth were given to her. She hated them and threw them away.

Some days her mind was so clear and she thought about why she hadn't died that day. Better yet, why hadn't she killed her husband? She would have gone to prison and be out on good behavior by now. After all this time, the pain of what he did to her was still so powerful in her heart. She shook her head to try and clear her mind. She could not get away from her own thoughts. Over and over they screamed in her head.

Gracie walked over to the chair and sat. She could hear voices outside her room. Someone was always begging for a smoke. Life with her inmates, she thought to herself and smiled. They were crying, yelling, or cursing out one another. The smells were nauseating: someone either smelled of urine or vomit or their own filth. Like her they were lost souls. They were supervised, watched, fed, and medicated but no one held their hand and listened to their needs, wants, or desires. No one comforted them or helped to erase and calm their fears. Objects to study, to dissect, is how they all were treated, Gracie believed.

There was her friend Joe, a good old Irish boy who was about ninety years old. He was very thin and dirty looking with his right hand always in his pants playing with himself. All day long his hand would come out of his pants he'd smell his fingers and then back into his pants his hand would disappear. A long time ago Gracie heard that he was an ex-Marine. Then there was Mary a black American who combed her hair all day long with a pick. Sadly, she had no hair. Her head was completely bald. For two cigarettes she would give anybody a sexual favor of their choice was the rumor. Gus on the other hand was neat as a pin. His hair was combed with a part straight as an arrow. He wore a tie every day since he'd been there. His suit was frayed and old but neat and clean. He never spoke one word that Gracie could recall. Rumor was that he couldn't speak. When the lights were out Gracie could hear him at night crying in the room next door. These were her friends that she had accumulated through the years. She shook her head from side to side as one single tear fell. They had nicknamed her "The Major!" She stood up for them if she was witness to any abuse from the aides, shared her money and candy with them, and tried in some way to comfort and listen to them. She was more aware than them of the rights they still possessed. After all, they were not criminals; they had not committed any crimes except for misplacing their minds as she teased them.

Closing her eyes she was capable of escaping, to travel to the mansions of her mind bringing up moments that still seemed so real to her. It had been a crisp cool night, right after many days of rain. Gracie felt alone that night and sad. Earlier Rob had screamed at her to get herself together; she was always a mess when he came home. The house now empty and silent, she had to admit she was having trouble dealing with the feeling of no longer being needed. The children were gone and grown and he was always working. When she walked out of the shower the answering machine was blinking and she heard his message: "Another night of working late, see you in the morning." She decided to go to Barnes & Noble and buy him a present; he loved to read as much as her, a bond they shared as they discussed the books they read at one time in front of the fireplace with a glass of wine.

At first, she was startled when she saw him walking hand and hand with a small blonde coming out of the movies. Then she heard him laugh. His laugh that was for only her she had believed. Like a knife his voice pierced her heart. From that moment on she was never the same. She believed that literally at that exact moment her heart broke open and she lost her mind completely. It was his laugh that pushed her over the edge.

She noticed cars were blowing their horns at her but she just walked out of her car in a trance towards Rob. She stood in front of them, as he walked side by side with the blonde together and simply, quietly said, "Hi." Rob froze as shock filled his eyes. Gracie looked into them and knew that he no longer loved her. In his eyes she saw guilt and relief. She ran to her car. She didn't know what she expected from him but imagined that he would have run after her. He did not.

Gracie pulled into the first parking lot because of the pain in her chest and the tears that were blinding her eyes. She sat for hours thinking and re-thinking her life. The children were both grown and no longer living with them; she cried harder for the loss she felt inside. The emptiness inside that she had somehow missed her own life. Where had she been all these years? Wasn't this the time she read of in books where they would begin again? Free to explore and travel as the magazines told her. She felt the betrayal within her entire body. She knew she needed some kind of answers and that he would be waiting for her at home. She was afraid to face him and to hear what he had to say, but on the other hand she wanted to know – she wanted to know everything.

Tortured by her own thoughts and sad! She felt like she had just received a beating, her whole body ached. She knew how deeply she loved him but to learn that he no longer loved her was crippling her. There he stood at the window in their den with his back to her.

Before he could talk, she had to know:

"DO YOU LOVE HER?" she screamed.

He didn't turn around, but very quietly whispered:

"Yes."

Gracie tried to control herself; he was never one for screaming matches, and she needed to know what had happened to them.

"That's all you have to say is yes? Your one word has shattered my life, broken my heart, and ended our marriage."

Rob looked at her now, dropping his head, as if to rest his chin on his chest as he began.

"Gracie, I've no answers to give you except that it's over, our life together as we have known it. It ended for me a long time ago. To be honest with you it is a relief that you found out."

Gracie felt frozen in time; her head throbbed as her heart smashed into pieces at the sound of his calm voice. Her body shook uncontrollably and for a second Gracie felt like she would be sick. Her head grew foggy and she couldn't think. She wanted to stop and go back to before this pain. She turned now and stumbled out of the room.

It had been so long ago this nightmare she lived through. Still the pain sizzled in her veins. She crumbled that night because the only love that she trusted had not been true in the end. Who was this stranger to her that he now loved another? He had stated a fact with no thought to the pain a simple word like "yes" can create. He had been her whole life. The realization that he was able to love another besides her cut like a knife through her entire body. She trusted him and placed him before all other men as an honest and faithful one.

To learn he had been capable of lying and betraying her was even still unbelievable after all of these years. Gracie wiped the tears from her eyes as she returned to her mind and began to relive the moments that set her up for eternity.

She stood in their beautiful white marble bathroom with the 18K gold Kohler fixtures until confusion and voices blurred her vision. To this day, she saw herself standing at the sink with a razor in her right hand. Voices – she heard voices, over and over again they taunted her. "Rob does not love you anymore; your mother never loved you, and nobody will ever love you." There was no pain; she saw what she imagined was her skin in the sink and red water that must have been her blood. Her neck felt wet and her wrist was bloody. That was when she panicked and decided to leave the house clutching her blouse around her neck. As she started to walk downstairs she saw Rob was approaching her. He saw her pale face and how she clutched the blouse, which was bloody to her neck. "Gracie," he screamed, "what have you done?" Tears pouring down her face mixed with the blood from her wrist and neck she barely whispered, "I only loved you," then collapsed.

An ambulance would take her to the hospital and she would be sewed up and placed in a psychiatric ward. Gracie died that night but continued to live. She remembered afterwards this feeling that she had imagined that she would learn a life lesson that would calm her soul and fulfill her reason for being and why she did indeed not die that night. Was this a dream she dreamed of on the operating table or just a feeling?

Then it began – hospitals, doctors, even police were called in. Gracie was labeled and told she was mentally ill. She had tried to commit suicide by slicing her throat and wrist with a razor blade. For the rest of her life she would be crippled in her left hand. She would glance down at it over the years and to her it resembled a claw of some kind. To Gracie it didn't belong to her body. Open and close, it could go on a will of its own. She could not make it function ever again as her other hand. A reminder of a night she could never get away from. She had been forty years old when she tried to truly end it. All because she could not imagine living without his love or trying to live with his betrayal!

After that night, she never could get it together again. She did try but she always ended up back in an institution. They called these little episodes nervous breakdowns. After awhile, she lost count of the many times she was locked up and released, locked up and released. What did it matter? For years she had felt like a zombie from another planet. Eventually, he divorced her. When it turned out that Gracie was not going to get better ever, and was to be institutionalized for the rest of her life, Amanda became her angel.

A pattern formed and on a regular basis Amanda visited her or took her out for the day on a pass. They talked and spoke about life and a bond grew that warmed Gracie's insides. Her son was busy living his own life in another state, controlled by his wife instead of his mother. He never was able to handle or accept Gracie's illness.

Gracie shook her head; she didn't want to think of the rest. She took off her sunglasses and rubbed her eyes. In her room she was safe only because no one could see inside her soul. To actually be witness and see the pain that was within. At times these memories and travels to the mansions of her mind exhausted her on a daily basis. His betrayal was the end of her. For Gracie that was what life was about: the dream of true love and a normal life, which she craved, that was never to be. It came down to the fact that Gracie had found a way to remove her pain. Her medication made life simple. Only she knew the true diagnosis was lack of love. She needed to believe that she was loved. She had wanted to die that night and accepted that in reality she was no longer alive. Gracie could not understand why her mother could not love her and then her husband stopped loving her too.

After dinner she lay down on her bed with the door open to think of the days that flew by yearly. The weeks were intertwined with one another. Somewhere along the line she became a grandmother, and there were parties and holidays she was allowed passes for. She told herself she was different and she didn't belong in the real world anymore. She did crave what that simple word family stood for. She knew how to behave and be on her best behavior when she was let out.

Amanda would tell her, "Clean yourself up, take off the junk, the rosaries, the plastic beads," that she loved to wear. The junk, as her daughter referred to the jewelry she wore, made her smile. She would pick things up off the street and make them her own. It didn't matter that it was old or dirty plastic. What mattered was that it belonged then to her. Amanda would tell her to "watch how you act in front of the children, control yourself, or I won't pick you up and bring you to my house." Gracie was proud of Amanda and the strength she had as a mother and a woman. She knew that it was not Amanda that cared how she appeared or what she wore but it was her husband who worried about what others would think.

One day she couldn't handle going there and then having to return to "the institution," and she told her, "I don't belong in your world; it confuses and upsets me to go from where I live to a normal household and then to return to the world of the lost." This is where I belong, she told herself and Amanda. Gracie had accepted her existence finally.

Then the routine changed and her daughter would visit once a week to bring her smokes, candy, and spending money. Gracie fell into her world now with utter abandonment and at times forgot to change her clothes or bathe when Amanda visited. Amanda would not be able to control her face and would ask, "Why are you so dirty? Why do you have food stuck to your blouse and your hands and your nails are filthy too? You have to clean yourself up daily!" Gracie would smile and say to her, "I'm sorry, I forgot, can you give me $5 more today?" she would plead. Amanda's face would soften and she would give Gracie whatever she wanted or needed.

Gracie knew that Amanda figured out she gave money to her friends who had no one. Her daughter would try to be mad at her and tell her, "The money is for you – do not give it away." Sometimes Gracie was out of money before the week was up and Amanda would run over early to see her. Gracie liked to see her and didn't really care about the money; she just needed to see her for a bit. Through the years Amanda never stopped coming and visiting her.

She found a deep love inside for her daughter and tried now to speak to her about everything. Sometimes she would pull up in her convertible and Gracie would jump in; they would blast the radio and drive through the neighborhood. She loved the wind in her face and when she closed her eyes she was not Gracie, the mentally ill one; she was alive, happy, and living a great life. Those were the special pass days when Gracie was let out. Gracie would store the day in a secret place for she was always creating new memories to travel to later.

She missed seeing her grandchildren but in the end felt it was better than them seeing her so different from others. It was easier for Gracie to be insane daily than to be sane for a few hours in front of them. Somewhere along this path he had re-married but she stored that information far away from her mind.

Another day, another night, as memories filled her, she relaxed in her bed drifting away to the mansions of her mind. Doors would open and there she would be in another place and time. She could feel the tears welling up in her eyes. For almost six months, at one time she had lived on disability like a real person in the real world. That was a time in her life she would never forget because of the depth of her sorrow.

She saw herself now sitting on the bed, watching television, eating candy and potato chips. Her daughter came once a week with food and would clean for her. One day she had heard voices telling her to write. So she did – on the walls with different color crayons. It looked so pretty to her. A work of art she thought. She remembered now writing all day and how happy she felt. For the life of her she couldn't recall where the crayons came from. Maybe her daughter had visited with the grandchildren one day? Why was it important for her to remember this? Her mind played tricks on her always taking her back. She recalled then another day the voices told her to take off her clothes and walk outside. To look at the sun and let the warmth cover her body like a blanket. She always listened to the voices for they knew her best. When she was arrested and brought back to her room the landlord saw her writings on the walls. Her daughter was called and she ended up back in an institution. That was the time in her life where she was at a crossroads. She had been given a second chance she liked to believe. Sadly for Gracie she took the wrong road and ended up dependent on the beliefs of society.

During that time she remembered how sad and frightened Amanda looked when she visited. Gracie tried to protect her from the other "crazies," as they got in her face screaming, "Got a smoke? Got a smoke?" She would push them away and yell, "She's here to visit me – get away!" They would then sit for a few hours and talk. Gracie was witness to an inner beauty whenever Amanda spoke of her children. She filled with love for this daughter that she herself had neglected at one time as she shared her thoughts with her over the years.

In the distant mansions of her mind calmly she lay in her bed now as another door opened. She was standing in a room, as their eyes met across the moonlit gardens. She could smell sweet flowers by her side. Her body became frozen as she stared into his jet-black eyes. This butterfly feeling in her stomach was one that only Rob could stir up. She was at an affair for one of her grandchildren. Then it dawned on Gracie that Rob was walking towards her. One more second and they would be together again for the first time in years. She stretched out her hand for him to shake – instead he pulled her into his arms and hugged her tightly. For a split second she felt safe again after all that they had been through. She could stay in his arms forever and dream that she was still his wife. How did she not imagine he would be here too? Stupid of her! She tried to focus on what he was saying but she felt all fogged up. She saw his glance look at her from the top of her head to her feet as he said, "Hi Gracie, how are you? You look well and very happy!"

Gracie thought inside her head, he thinks I look sane. Thank God she listened to Amanda and let her buy her a new dress for the party. Gracie smiled to herself; she wanted Amanda to be proud of her and actually had been able to lose some weight by not eating all the junk and just giving it away. She smiled holding back the tears as she answered him, "Rob, I'm fine and doing well. Medication does wonders for people like me. Don't you agree? You look great too, how are you doing?"

As they stood facing one another panic filled her throat as if she would begin to cry. The little voice in her head demanded that she control herself and take in as much as possible of him. DO NOT WEAKEN! Out of the corner of her eye she saw the blonde approaching them. Panic was taking over. She had to leave before the girl came any closer. She heard her own voice shake as she whispered, "Rob, I have to go now; you'll never know how much I really loved you." She turned and walked away before he could answer her. She felt hollow and empty and scared even after all this time at the memory. That was the end of her thinking she could handle the real world. She ended up where she is at this very moment in a world that did not exist to anyone but people who stumble through the cracks of life.

Gracie opened her eyes. She was tired of all the years of dreaming. He had always told her she was a dreamer. She had been dreaming of the past and life had passed her by. Laughter filled her head because she was still alive after all the dreams and nightmares. How much longer would she exist like this continuing day after day, night after night, year after year, with these mansions that filled her mind? Violently she shook her head as she had done so many times before to rid herself of her own thoughts.

Gracie believed that everyone has a purpose and path in life to follow. She noticed that her thoughts were more recently about Amanda and an inner love she was feeling. Amanda never stopped visiting her and at times she had to tell her, "Go home to your family." Could there possibly be a person that truly loved Gracie after all?

Slowly she walked toward the dresser and pulled out the bottom drawer. In the drawer there was a white envelope that was starting to turn yellow. Inside of it was a small tattered picture almost destroyed from her constantly touching it every day when she would look at the picture! Also in the envelope were several pieces of paper she had kept to read over and over.

A long time ago she had begun to write poetry about her mind, her loves, her beliefs, and her sorrows. These were her two sole possessions that she treasured. Except for the envelope the dresser was empty. She gently touched the face of the little girl in the picture. She knew she no longer looked as innocent and young but she believed the sadness in the eyes had never left. A single tear slipped out of her eye as she touched her lips to the little girl's face as she had done many times before. Her heart ached for this little lost girl that had grown to be an old lost woman. A sigh escaped her as she fumbled to open a small piece of paper as she began to read one of her poems:

A Tear

Their faces the same,
As they look about!
They are in a room,
And can't get out!
Their minds begin to shout!
No one listens.
No one hears.
There is sadness everywhere,
Then you see a tear.
They have no where to go
Their world is so slow
They only exist.
And never insist.

Chapter Six

Acceptance

Gracie was amazed at herself. She had lived for the past thirty years on the government. They fed and clothed her, as well as medicated her. She had wanted for nothing all of these years (ha-ha) and they say she's crazy! Time had slipped right through her fingers. The pain was buried deep down in her gut. She existed on yesterday all of these years. Somewhere, somehow, she had calmed herself. Her spirit accepted the existence she chose. Her mind fought on a daily basis with her. The mansions of her mind got her through life. She finally accepted that she belonged somewhere. Throughout the years it seemed to Gracie she was capable of helping others. She was there for those who had no one.

The routine of her daughter visiting her and bringing her items she needed had lasted. Ironically the one person she tried desperately to not love ended up being the one who loved her the most. The pattern of her life had carried on but her daughter was even stronger than her and refused to be pushed away. Today she was turning seventy years old. Amanda was coming at 11 o' clock and she knew she would have with her a banana split. Gracie would not have made it if it had not been for her daughter, she told herself that now.

Their roles had reversed it seemed to Gracie somewhere through the years; at times she felt like Amanda was her mom. Her own heart had softened towards her daughter. Through the years she always tried to upset her and at times found herself actually mean to her but Amanda never stopped coming. After thirty years of being ill and living in an institution, an adult home, and then back in an institution, the one love in Gracie's life was her daughter today.

The mansions of Gracie's mind were still her escape to yesterday and what had been. Slowly she rose from the bed, knowing she had to get ready for Amanda's visit. She felt old and run down. Her knees hurt, making it difficult to walk. She had also acquired a hacking cough. On a monthly basis a medical doctor checked her blood levels and examined her. After all these years on different medications she was always proud to tell her daughter that she was physically fit. They would laugh together and at the same time say "but not mentally fit." In a few weeks she was due for her annual checkup. One at an institution waited, Gracie had learned over time. You needed to fill out a form for everything.

She sat down to wait for Amanda as she adjusted her sunglasses again, drifting off to a long time ago, when she was told that her son had been killed in a car crash. A stupid kind of accident Gracie always felt. While walking across Main Street USA, Rob Jr. was hit by a drunk driver. He died instantly. That was a very sad day bringing forth memories of being a mom and a housewife. Wrenching tears fell from her eyes at the thoughts that filled her head that sad day. It was also the last time she ever saw her husband. Older like her but still able to take her breath away, the love she felt for him that day still flowed through her veins. She knew that she loved him more than her own life as she watched him from a distance. She had the proof of this love all around her every day in her mind. Watching him she saw a spark of sadness in his eyes that she was never able to erase from her own memory.

Here they were burying their son! For the first time in her life she saw Rob cry uncontrollably. She herself felt numb and out of her element. The entire family and all their friends had come to bury her son. Gracie felt that they also came to see how she reacted. How the mental person looked. She couldn't believe that she knew so many people. Her cousins from long ago arrived to pay their respects yet never once had they visited Gracie. She had wondered to herself at the funeral, where had all these people been all of these years? Was Gracie that far removed from the real world? Amanda had cleaned her up and told her to behave and not make a scene. Of course she listened; she did not want to upset Amanda. As long as she could wear her sunglasses she was happy and felt safe.

Gracie vowed that day to never attend another burial of anybody that she knew. She didn't care who died. Everybody was carrying on as if they knew or cared for her son, when he had lived out of state for years. No one even saw him most of the time, except Amanda. No one cared when he was alive – why cry now? Gracie believed that you had to be good to people while they were alive and not be sorry after they were dead. She didn't believe in going to the cemetery and praying over a grave either. Gracie may have been considered mentally ill but she had her beliefs. She knew in her heart that we are put here to learn from one another. To be good and love one another! Not just to say empty words of love but to show love for each other. For Gracie it had always been about the action and doing part of life. The little things mattered most to her. The memories of yesterday that could put a smile on her face. Her memories kept her going. She believed in the afterlife and that if one did right peace would be yours for the taking. If one did wrong they were thrown back into the pit to get it right.

Seeing Rob that day was to last her the rest of her lifetime. He was still beautiful to her. She had hugged him back, but what could they really say to one another? Today wasn't about them. They spoke with their eyes. Together they remembered the little boy, the moments stored away from yesterday. They hadn't shared a life together for over twenty years. Still their bond held strong, they were parents of a child that needed to be buried. After today Rob would continue living his life and Gracie would return to the institution. That was a fact she accepted. That was the message they passed to each other with their eyes.

She heard voices in the hall. She shook herself away from yesterday and there stood Amanda with her banana split. Chocolate candy and ice cream were her favorites. Amanda always brought her candy but today was special, being that it was her birthday. As she looked at her daughter she felt an enormous wave of love towards her. She was older herself now with bits of gray in her hair but beautiful as Gracie smiled at her. She marveled at the style her daughter possessed and the endurance she showed the world. Amanda had become a mom herself years ago and was a very good one. Gracie would tease her when they were together and refer to her also as her "mom." To Gracie Amanda had become the ideal mom figure that she herself had always searched for.

Gracie felt her mind drifting away from it all to the past. Amanda's children were grown now but years ago Gracie had connected with them. Like Amanda they had no fear of Grammy, as they called her, and found her really funny. How did her daughter become such a good mom when she had walked away from her all those years ago? Could it be true that we all try desperately not to become our parents? In the end though Gracie knew blood and love was the connection. She could see the manic-behavior in her son when he was younger. She heard through the years about his sons and how troubled they were. All from the same household but lost in their own nightmares. The older one grew up to be a real estate lawyer. The middle son became a drug addict who would die of an overdose. The youngest, a builder of fine furniture, who loved to work with his hands, formed his own company.

"MOM, MOM," yelled Amanda, "where are you? I brought you a present from the children. A box filled with Hershey's Kisses because they're your favorite and some butterscotch sucking candies that the children wanted you to know they picked out special for you. They always remembered that you would visit them and dig in your pocket until you pulled out candy for them to eat when they were small."

Gracie smiled, her grandchildren remembered her by a little action she shared with them. It had always been the little things for Gracie. She was happy as she said, "I love it! I love the candy and I can't wait to sit down, watch television, and devour it all. Tell them every time I pop a Kiss into my mouth I'll think of them. Thank them for the great birthday present and memories."

Amanda stayed for about three hours and when she left they hugged and kissed like they had been doing all of these years. Gracie lay down on the top covers of her bed. No sleeping in the daytime they were told constantly. If she stayed above the covers they left her alone. The mansions of her mind were bursting with yesterday. Her grandchildren never really knew her. Even though she spent time with them as babies, the time would come when they would only have their own memories of her, which she saw today, she accomplished by their gift of candy they sent.

In the past whether she saw them or not she left them a gift. A little gift! Bazooka bubble gum sometimes or a handful of butterscotch was her favorite. Chocolate Kisses melted in your mouth and they were bite size. They would laugh at her and ask to see her mouth. Grammy had no teeth. They would ask her, "How do you eat? What do you eat? Doesn't it hurt? Where are your teeth?" Gracie laughed at the memories. Her answer was always the same. "I lost my teeth and I suck and gum all my food until it becomes mush." They would scream together, "Yucky!"

They really didn't care about her teeth; they wanted to see how she ate the candy. Gracie would then show them. In amazement they would sit at her feet and would watch her open a piece of candy, then open her mouth as they looked in to make sure the teeth were still not there. She would place the candy on her tongue and suck it in, making loud noises as the candy melted in her mouth. Once again they would ask, "Open up Grammy, and let us see in." Sometimes she made them believe her mouth was stuck and they would laugh hysterically. When she opened her mouth the candy would be gone. They would scream, "Let us try!" That was the part Gracie liked the best. They would all get a piece of candy and try not to use their teeth to eat it. Of course, they were young and couldn't control themselves. It became a game and something they could share. Over and over they would sit there taking turns trying to eat the candy and not use their teeth. In the end the candy would be gone, and it would be time for Gracie to leave.

Gracie felt her face was wet and she hadn't realized she'd been crying. The older she was getting, the tears came quicker and unannounced. She removed her sunglasses and wiped her eyes with the sleeve of her shirt. Today she was seventy years old. She felt she was lucky to have her own mind to escape to all of these years. She could lay here forever reliving her own life. She needed a smoke at this moment. She rose up from the bed and walked over to the window. The window was still dirty but the sun was shining and she could almost see the blue sky above. Gracie loved to stand for hours and watch the sun, rain, or snow. The beauty of nature was what she missed most of all. To feel the warmth of the sun's rays on her face or the cool water of raindrops hitting her head had always delighted her in the past. Just to walk in the snow and make a snowball excited her at one time.

With trembling hands that always shook now, she lit her cigarette. Inhaling deeply she felt the smoke drift inside her body filling her lungs. When she exhaled she choked and began to cough. This dam hacking cough drove her crazy. That thought put a smile on her lips. She sat down in her chair waiting for the coughing to be over. Closing her eyes she remembered when Amanda came to tell her that her mother had died. She didn't feel anything. She didn't cry. She didn't feel sad. It was as if a stranger had died. Her own mother had died alone in her empty house while watching television. She simply slipped out of life, a very comfortable death Gracie imagined. Was this a gift from God to not let her suffer anymore? After all, she was full of pain during her life and inflicted pain on her own child, which Gracie believed must have been enough for her to live through. Gracie had been her only child and she never loved Gracie or was part of her life. When Gracie was first hospitalized her mother never once came to visit her. She had at one time called Amanda to tell her that she prayed every night that Gracie would die so that Amanda could get on with her own life and not have the responsibility of caring for Gracie. Amanda herself had not known her grandmother, so she felt protective towards Gracie and imagined how ill this strange woman must have been herself to wish her own child dead.

Gracie and Amanda thought the same when it came to life and the living. The foundation they lived by was that one is responsible for their life and how they treat others. Gracie tried her best to love and be loved. The desperation of no love from her mother to a husband who could just walk away from her shattered her being.

She could think back to a lifetime ago when her dad held her hand that day and took her to her grandmother's house. That memory filled her with love for him. That memory could make Gracie cry for herself and her loss at his early death. That emotion even after sixty-five years could upset her and bring back the empty feeling when he died. Gracie had loved her father deeply. Gracie had loved Rob madly. Gracie never was given the chance to love her mother but she carried a special kind of love hidden inside her heart for the mother she craved her to be. Her father had left her the same day her mother had left but he was aware that as a child Gracie still needed to feel loved.

He showered her with love the best way he knew how. The little things in life were what mattered in the end. The park, the pool, and beach were all memories that were given to her by her father as he shared the wonders and beauties of nature with Gracie. Those were her cherished memories of her father today.

She could recall when she had begged her mother when she was older to be a part of her life. Her mother screamed at her words that she felt were knives going straight into her heart: "YOU'RE ACTING LIKE A BABY! LEAVE ME ALONE AND GROW UP! DON'T YOU KNOW THAT I NEVER WANTED YOU? I WISH YOU WERE NEVER BORN!" That day was a turning point in Gracie's young life. She looked at her mother with fresh eyes. She saw too much pain in her face and fear. She would store her love away because a child loves a mother no matter what.

Within a month of her mother's outburst Rob surfaced and to Gracie he was sent from the heavens above. To Gracie he was an Angel sent to rescue her from her pain and unloved life. Perfect timing, Gracie had thought back then. She needed to be loved and here he was willing and able to love her. The sadness could still fill her heart and make her shiver. He was the love of her life. He had betrayed her. He too has now been placed back in the vault of her mind because the empty feeling his memories stirred up could hurt her too much. She wanted to remember the husband she loved and the good times they had shared as a couple. Through the years she learned how to control her trips to her mansions and placed him as a thought for certain times.

Now she lived in the present and created a world with her daughter that she could escape to. For Amanda's sake she could imagine what their life together as husband and wife would be like today. They would be old together with gray hair and grandchildren. On Sundays they would have family dinner and as the proud grandparents babysit for Amanda. Gracie's mind could always dream of the past and what could have been. Gracie laughed to herself, yes, she was diagnosed manic-depressive, and at times she felt saner than the sane people she knew.

Gracie was always impressed with the mansions of her mind. She chuckled because she spent so much time escaping there. All she had to do is sit or lie quietly somewhere and the movie would begin playing. She had the lead role along with the other cast members of her life in the background. Recently her supporting actress was Amanda. These episodes could be of a happy time, a sad time, or a crazy time in her life. It definitely would be a time that Gracie had lived through. The medication and the people she lived with accepted her for what she was. She fit in perfectly. If she wanted, Gracie knew she could fit in perfectly in the real world. She just did not want to bother with the hassle of it all. People expected so much from each other. Gracie lived in the world God had chosen for her to learn from. This she accepted years ago entirely as her life was meant to be. She accepted it and lived it, drawing comfort from it.

Basically through the years Gracie's days were quiet and once a week Amanda would visit with stories of the children and candy. Gracie tried to share all she had with her friends and those who were alone. At one time she realized she was no longer alone because God was within and she was loved by Amanda. This realization that Gracie was no longer alone made life meaningful to her. As she existed she learned of all that her mind had to offer to her.

She listened when Amanda talked and saw a part of her silent as she herself had once been. Amanda devoted herself to her husband and children, erasing a part that was very important to her. This was the part that Gracie realized she could help Amanda with after all these years of Amanda staying by her side. She saw the strength and the goodness as love glowed in Amanda's eyes when she spoke of them. Her own dreams and needs were placed on hold as she cared and created and nourished everyone else. Was this the path of women of today? Gracie had lived through years and years of abuse herself and look where she ended up. She wanted more for Amanda and knew exactly what to do.

During the night Gracie felt very cold and wet. She didn't understand why no one was coming to help her, feeling very confused and unable to determine whether she was dreaming or in truth in her bed in the dark feeling extremely ill. When the aide finally came in to check on Gracie it was morning. Gracie was in a mess. She was hot with fever. She had urinated on herself, as well as dirtied her body and bed with diarrhea. An ambulance was called and she was rushed to the emergency room.

For hours she lay in her dirty clothes on a bed in the hall. She was treated differently because she was "from that place." Being considered insane has its disadvantages, Gracie thought to herself. Most of them had no family that would make waves if they were mistreated. It had been six o'clock in the morning when she was taken and now at one o'clock in the afternoon she still had not seen a doctor. She was scared, alone, and not feeling well. In walked Amanda and started yelling at everyone. Quiet, scared Amanda could do for Gracie what she could not do for herself. Within minutes she was cleaned up and given some water. Gracie felt the tears as they slid down her face. God had given her Amanda and she was very grateful. Blood was taken and an examination would tell Gracie that she had pneumonia.

The cough, the smoking, and the years of neglect had caught up with her. The hardest part about being in the hospital was "NO SMOKING." Amanda came every day, fed her, and sat with her. Sometimes she would bring ice cream and candy for her. They would watch television and talk about life and the years that were over and the ones coming.

Gracie was to learn she had lung cancer. The kind they called oat cell, which was inoperable. Gracie begged Amanda to make sure she would not be in pain. Her biggest fear was pain. She was terrified of needles and pain. Amanda promised to take care of her and visit every day. She met with a social worker because Gracie had to be removed from the institution into a nursing home.

Her daughter looked scared and confused but kept her promise and visited every day. She felt how afraid Amanda was. She tried to comfort her by telling her that she lived a good life and knew her time was up. At one point she told her that she too would die one day. Everyone gets to die. Amanda would laugh and look at her with love in her eyes. She had to have CAT scans, MRIs, and more blood work done before they started chemotherapy. In quick sharp words the doctor told Gracie she would live about six months if she did not take the chemotherapy, compared to another five years if she chose the chemotherapy.

These were special times now that the end was near and Gracie could have anything she wanted. The best part of the day was when Amanda pushed her around in a wheelchair, especially if they were able to go outside. Amanda promised to take her to see the movie Titanic when she was feeling better. She felt loved by Amanda and at times screamed for her to go home and take care of her family. Gracie realized her life would end and Amanda would feel lost.

Living in a nursing home Gracie was treated differently, as if she were sane. Being that she could no longer walk, she ate most of her meals in bed. She was allowed to stay in bed and be even under the covers. The mental institution was not capable of taking care of her any longer. This made Gracie laugh. She had been locked up for thirty years. The locks were open now and she had only one thing left that stayed the same. Her precious mansions of her mind could go with her anywhere.

She spent most of her time now in bed or if someone took her out and put her in a wheelchair. The saddest part for her was that she was dependent on someone to lift her in and out of bed to go to the bathroom or just sit in her wheelchair. So many times they simply would forget and she had to wait to be put back in bed. Cold and tired she would sit in the hall and just wait patiently. The hardest part was the night when the sounds of crying and emptiness filled the halls. So many of the ones on Gracie's floor were older than her and had no one to visit them. They were forgotten and cried out to whoever would listen as they tried to remember that they were people with dreams of their own at one time. Gracie would try to talk to them during the day, play cards, or just watch them go up and down the hall strapped in their wheelchairs.

Gracie cleaned her sunglasses as she drifted back to yesterday. Back to her days shared with Rob when they were in love and he brought her special presents. One time he had brought home from work the cutest little poodle. This was before the children were born when they were in love and would escape to different little hideaways they found through the years in secluded beaches. She never quite understood what had happened so long ago. She had never meant to become ill and to be institutionalized eventually.

Gracie felt that everyone was given a plan. This she then believed had been her destiny. She thanked God every night for all that was part of her life. She had loved painting at one time and classical music and was fascinated by Hollywood and the movie business. Would it ever have been a consideration that she would have lived a different type of life? Gracie didn't think so for in the pit of her stomach she felt safe now. She felt loved by Amanda.

Now that she looked back she saw the manic Gracie from yesterday walking sometimes eighteen hours through the streets searching for something. Those were the times she herself could not control her actions. Had it always been about the nightmares that filled every waking hour for Gracie? The mind she was not capable of controlling back then. She would acquire this energy like no other and go and go and go. Yet she never accomplished anything but looking and acting insane. She had the need to write and be heard anywhere and on any subject. She blew up to over two hundred pounds and then went down to under one hundred pounds. Life had been an enormous experience for Gracie and that was a fact.

Today Gracie's mind was different. She was taken off her regular medication because of the chemotherapy. She herself felt different, almost normal. Was that possible? She still had the ability to escape into her mansions only because she felt safe there. The doctors questioned her daily and she looked at them as if they were insane, not her. Stupid questions she would tell Amanda that she refused to answer.

"How do you feel? What day is today? Do you know your name? Who is the President of the United States?"

Gracie's answers were always the same.

"How do I look? Why, you don't know what day it is? Aren't you the doctor? Do you know your name? Is that where I am in the United States?"

They would tell Amanda that her mind was getting worse and that they were going to have to sedate Gracie. Amanda would yell at her to just answer the stupid questions and stop being a brat. Gracie felt bad for Amanda and could see that she was scared and tired. Gracie only had Amanda but she felt that this was too much of a strain on her to watch her mother actually die. "Go home," she would yell at her. Then she would pretend she was asleep.

The mansions were a novelty and a creation of hers to take her away. After all these years, who had ended up being the one who took care of her, the one who visited, the one and only one who loved her? Amanda she realized had shared her life with her, no questions asked. No recriminations that she was insane. A bond had formed between two women that filled her with pride and love as a mother towards a daughter. Pride and love which had been missing in her life as a daughter herself had been offered to her with open arms from Amanda.

In the end Gracie, confused and medicated, believed the answer was a simple one after all. Love is the glue in life that makes all things possible connecting people to one another. Did Amanda realize the love and support she had showered on Gracie? Gracie saw the young quiet Amanda now. Her father's little girl she had always been. Yet, in the end it was her daughter who truly cared. Out of all the people who had crossed Gracie's path in life, the sane, the insane, the good, and some of them had been troubled, she had spent the last thirty years of her life and probably even before she was ill loved by her daughter. The mind is a tricky place and Gracie jumbled hers up until she ran away from reality to protect her heart. She was not capable of living without love. The mansions of her mind were a way she could continue to live and dream.

All those years Gracie favored her son. Her son had left her long before his death. He had been scared away by Gracie. He was terrified of becoming like her. They shared laughter and moments where Gracie always told him he was just like her. How silly to think in that manner and in reality scaring a child. Fear had set in early in her son's life. He tried to hide behind a bottle of booze to erase the fears within. In the past she had heard the stories from Amanda about his abusive behavior with his own family. The drinking with his buddies late at night after work became a need to run away from his own life. The physical and mental abuse he inflicted on his family saddened Gracie through the years when Amanda visited. Yesterday, the past, the memories, the foggy recollections – her mansions, her mind had been part of her life, her quiet existence, and her escape.

She smiled to herself because she had a gift for Amanda. Gracie had a secret. In the bottom drawer of her dresser was a collection of her thoughts, her writings on the wall so to speak, that she was leaving for her. Being ill had been a full-time job for Gracie and Amanda. Whenever she had a chance she wrote. There was always an attendant or nurse that would help her keep her secret from Amanda. Even now the nurse would help her with her papers when she could no longer get out of bed. Reading over her words at one time filled her with sadness. She had been depressed, lonely, scared at times, and angry. Just like she was capable of escaping into the mansions, she escaped into the written word. Her writings were a form of confession for her. It cleansed her soul and spirit to put on paper the words she felt in her heart. Gracie tried now to remember the simple words she wrote through the years. A little story sort of explaining her wants, her needs, her loves, and her desires! Things no one ever gets to speak out loud to anybody. She wished that she could be here with Amanda to see her reaction when she learns of the person who was her mother.

Gracie knew that she was experiencing the last mansion of her mind as she lay down and closed her eyes. She hadn't been out of bed for two weeks. The nurses were kind and would give her morphine whenever she said she was in pain. Amanda had just left after sitting with her all day. The room was dark and quiet as she began to drift off. In her mind she saw the larger-than-life Amanda. She was happy she was alone and that Amanda was home with her family where she belonged. She would get the telephone call and run back to the nursing home very sad and in pain. Gracie knew down deep in her heart Amanda would miss her tremendously for the rest of her life.

Slowly like in a haze she could see Amanda going through her dresser. She wanted to hold her hand and tell her, "Don't cry, darling, you were an excellent daughter. I thank you for the gift of love you bestowed on me. I am returning home and I will wait for you. You still have so much to do with your own life." In the fourth drawer tied together with a yellow ribbon lay her simple gift of words. Gracie smiled to herself as she floated farther and farther away. Her title page read: I was here! Where I am you shall be! Let my words set us free!

Amanda's heart ached with love and amazement. After all these years Gracie's story was written. She brought herself back to the months of when Gracie had first left her. Her own words had become therapy in her life for her too. Ironically Gracie believed in what Amanda feared for herself. She sat back down and began to write and decided to include the true gift of love Gracie had left her. Amanda believed that through love and belief they had become intertwined and created an entity that filled them with the love they both needed from each other. Wiping her tears away, she began to type the words she found left behind as a gift by Gracie for her.

Chapter Seven

Encourage

My dear Amanda,

Seventy years of torment and turmoil are enough for anyone. I chose the existence in this lifetime to be almost at the bottom of the barrel. Yet, my wisdom in an earlier lifetime shone through. Throughout my existence I believed that I had tried to right the wrongs of my life once before. In amazement I believe now that I finally found the answer and erased the need to return again. Remember, Amanda, the many talks about reincarnation that we shared. How we must learn to forgive and accomplish a life with love. At least we both agreed about that. The choices we get to choose ourselves. How exciting that it can really be this way. You chose me to be your mother so that we could learn together. Although, I did not know all that I would learn from you. How you would be the one to ease my pain in the end. I had started out troubled and filled with fear but in the end you comforted me.

To choose myself, a young mother to be my mom, when at the age of sixteen she gave birth to me, and filled me with the pain and search of a lifetime. In my heart and troubled childhood I was always searching for that missing love only a mother bestows on her child. After being left at the early age of five by her, to be shuffled back and forth among relatives, I survived. *The man, the father, I chose to be my dad, was a kind, good, simple man who would die young and leave me to fend for myself. To pick the year 1927 to be born in New York City was brave of me. To live through a period of life with the changes that war brought, depression, the invention of color television, talking movies, electronics, the world finally growing into computers and pain caused by the death of many by the use of drugs were all mine to learn from. To not learn was my choice at one time. To be uneducated was par for the day back then, but wisdom was inside of me and this I would learn from you.*

My wisdom and beliefs to be true to myself, my goodness towards others, but the ability to love was my greatest quality. No matter how, who, or what I reincarnated to I had these attributes. I could not hide them. For they were me! Being a troubled, lonely, unloved child I grew up to be a very needy woman and abusive mother myself. Still, my past ways shone through to this lifetime. I could encourage. I could understand and love till it drove me mad.

In the middle of my life I decided to end my suffering during a weak moment but even that I could not accomplish. My lesson for the attempt on my own life was to live another thirty years in limbo and learn. At that time I felt as if I was forgotten and I needed to leave this world and move on. I began a search within for the reason I did not die because I was shocked that I still lived. I existed but I felt dead for a long time. I lived with other troubled, lost souls that nobody loved and spread my wisdom among them. I became a leader to them. I felt I needed them, as well as they needed me. In a way through the years they had become my family, these other troubled souls I lived with. I was an experiment for the drugs required to cure a mentally ill person. I was in a world I chose to learn about, to find the strength, the humility to know how the beaten soul survives. The world around me was harsh and at times scared me to the point of crying in the night in fear but there was always one light in my darkness.

When disease hit me and the cancer grew within I knew at one point I no longer would be in control. I knew the end would finally be near.

Waiting down the road was another journey and I knew it would be soon. I wanted to leave you with a simple gift after all the years you gave of yourself to me; a special gift for you which would enlighten you into my mind and explain my life. I thought of this a long time ago, as you will see from the words I used to try and erase my pain and sorrow for the mistakes I made. I have always been able to find comfort in the written word, whether my own or the knowledge I could gain from someone else. Thirty years is a long time to do nothing but dream and escape. So many times I sat and wrote after your visit but I never had the opportunity or the guts to show you these simple words of mine. There were so many times I wanted to tell you I was sorry for not being the mom you needed. I know how it feels to want to be loved by your mom.

I knew the time would come when I would lie in my hospital bed swollen and unable to communicate because of the drugs. I would wait for the outcome – death. I realized in my mind that now my learning was over, my pain was coming to an end.

Yes, through the years I learned…

How it felt to be unwanted and unloved; I cringe at the memory of abuse and the feeling of sorrow in my chest for that little girl that I had been. The little girl who existed among the living, yet they did not know she was there. Years I tried to find love and its substitute. Instead I became crazed and confused, locked away. The different medicines and miracle pills given to me never eased the pain of no love. I learned I could love and connect but only to one in the whole universe. This one was my light in the darkness and she gave me the gift of understanding, the strength to fault no one, the ability to forgive. For no matter how I tried to make her fear me, she refused. She stood strong and loved me as I was. She would not let me perish in this world, as if I had no one.

From the moment she was born to the moment I died, my daughter, yes you, Amanda, stood by my side, encouraging and accepting me as myself. Your greatest gift to all is your belief that everyone has the right to be their own person. To love unconditionally, to not demand anything from another, even if one feels unloved during life themselves.

Now my gift to you, Amanda, is my wisdom, my memory, and my love. You will carry the torch, the belief that it is possible to learn the reason we are here. Your road I know will be hard without me once I am gone. You have the calmness of my spirit and knowledge of my crazy beliefs to clear the path for you. Time and years will pass without me and you will remember many conversations we had about life, death, children, and the world as it is.

Amanda, out of seventy years of looking and searching and drowning in the world of no love you showed me how it felt to be loved. You stayed by my side. You loved me to my end. In my writings is a part of your mother you never knew. What goes on between husband and wife is a bond and secret of sorts. Life's journey is shared in marriage until one can no longer learn from the other. Someone is always bound to hurt deeper because of the pain inflicted on them from those who claim undying love. This is only because one always loves more than another. No loves can be the same. We forget to encourage and love each other, as we all must be. I let your father be true to himself through the years, because I was honored to be his wife and proud that he had chosen me. I had to escape to step away and search for who I was. He was never capable of letting me be the person I could be. Love is all we need, yet we abuse it and refuse it at times.

I am now letting you in on the words I have written because I did not have the understanding I have today back then. I was young and in love with the belief in my heart that your father had a right to control me because I never felt loved by another. In my mind I needed his love to survive. I believed he knew about life and loving. In doing this I somehow erased myself as far as anyone is capable of doing and still in reality be alive. I was misguided in my love and that I believed I was beneath another hurt me the deepest. We are all created alike and equal in God's eyes. Never forget that. Believe always that God loves us just as we are because He created us.

With all my respect, with all my love, how I wish you had been my mother, yet, in the end, the truth be told, I was your mother.

As you read on and see my daily jottings surface and become witness to a beaten woman, I hope you find your own voice. Amanda, you are unique and filled with the gift of love to share with the world. Share my words and sprinkle them with your own as an added treat. Follow your inner voice and as you listen you will be led to greatness. To be who we are destined to be fills us with love unconditionally.

Tears streaming down Amanda's face she stood up and stretched and felt the inner calm that Gracie offered her. Today she understood she was able to comprehend the makings of a book to be intertwined by their life experiences which brought a smile to her lips.

As she sat back down she gathered her mother's papers around her to be typed now as part of their story, Making Believers, the book which she felt strongly pulled to write. For her this gift that Gracie chose to leave her soothed her fears and like she always believed allowed the wisdom of her mother's words to enlighten her way in their poetic ability to hypnotize as well. For these daily jottings of her thoughts and words she used to express the struggles in her life were only the answers she searched for. Some might believe them to be ramblings of a crazy woman and the mansions of the mind that she escaped to. Read as you may and see what you can gather from one who simply searched for love. The ache of sadness can be shared today by me for I too await the outcome of tomorrow.

We are all witness to each other's beliefs and needs that must be gathered together with the ingredient of love. Gracie, my mother, is no different than another woman who has not been able to find love from another in life. It does not need to be just the love of a mother, father, or husband. Gracie as a child experienced the worst kind of pain: a mother who could not love her, a father who died too young, and then a husband who chose to no longer love her. As a young child she felt the early pangs of not being loved. To be asked to relive as an adult abuse from a man she madly loved and accepted all that he was capable of pushed her over the edge. Her words are those of a beaten woman that believes there has to be love out there for her.

First, she silenced herself in her marriage, then she escaped when that marriage was no more. Can we judge her? No! We have not walked in her shoes at all. I am her daughter and I hope you are witness to the likeness in our lives that I am sure is not only our doing but also there are those of you who have mansions in your mind that I bet you escape to from time to time. Just be honest and, like me, thank Gracie for sharing with us all how simple little things, truly – madly – deeply, make a difference in life. The foundation of all children must be without a doubt one that enables them to be able to touch, taste, and feel love from their parents. How different Gracie's life could have been by the simple foundation called love.

Gracie's Gift...

Save All My Writings!
A Book Is In The Making Through My Daughter...

I believed always that love is the answer, Amanda. I write to heal my bruised existence. All I want is to belong and know love. In the beginning I began by pouring my heart onto the written page poetically to release my pain by communicating in a manner towards your father. I do not want to confuse you, but I want you to know I did know how to love. I was consumed by a deep love for my husband because at one time I felt that he was the only one who loved me. And so I wrote to him ...

I am witness to the beauty of nature, water at the beach, birds in the air, trees ever so green. I could glow in the sun as it rises and become humble as it sets. The calm and stillness of the water, no birds are seen in the air. While the sun rises to its peak as trees stand tall, ever so strong. Love can never be wrong.

I live in the past and truly love my husband. I am in awe of this man. I am thankful of the love he gave to me. True love for me is that I love another, no matter how they act or treat me. The saying love is blind is a fact for me. For when we said, "I do," on a rainy day and the world seemed so gray, yes, I became your bride and the years have gone by. It amazes me that you are still at my side. Our children are here and we hold them so dear. I look forward to growing together year-to-year. I want to boast my love to all so that they can see you are my true love until I go above.

I have the greatest patience for I believe in tomorrow. Alone in my mind I always believed my eyes were the opening to my soul's pain within. *Despair fills me for I need an enormous amount of love to survive. I pray to God to show me why I have this emptiness inside. I dwell in the past and hope that the future will offer me comfort. I forget about today. Everyday I can forget to smell the freshness in the air. I search in your eyes to see that you really do care. I stop and wonder how our tomorrows will compare. I fill with despair for I can't wait until we're together somewhere. Is this wrong of me to miss you so?*

I am on a quest and the word cherish says it all for me. I can no longer handle pain. It has become unacceptable that I am not loved. I blame myself for no one loving me. I chose not to be stronger. To search for this girl I have lost I insist, for our marriage has been divided because I cannot stay as I am and exist. I feel the current inside of me ever so deep. I picture a river of love with wind flying all around me towards the angels above.

I am fighting the world of depression today. I have made mistakes and fill with pain because of them. This man I love is so strong and silent at times. I feel I am weak as I hope to be free of my pain. I need to learn from the past mistakes. My life must not become about hate. Depression is a constant fight for me. I must shake it off and be free. My life has not been filled with pride as my eyes begin to open wide.

My soul is reaching out to hug me today, to comfort me to see that a change is desperately needed in my life. Life is about lessons, yet we choose to extinguish them and believe it is not possible to change. Foolish that I believe I need to live a life filled with pain. I know the pattern of life has been set before my time was ever a question. Can I somehow believe to make a difference with a suggestion? Once I became an adult I tried to strive to accomplish the change I needed to make. In the end could this erase the pain of heartache? Around and around, year after year, as I know it I need some assistance. Kindness and love can be a special part of my dignity. Unfortunately, I refuse to listen to the cries in my head I hear steadily. There is always tomorrow, I believe, but it too will simply just leave. I know it will be too late, the change will not come, and I will begin to grieve.

I am sorry for the years I tortured my family. Those were the times I could not control my actions, my tears, even my laughter. My cries for help were misunderstood. I so much wanted to be the mom that I myself searched for. Then I believed you were better off without me. Amanda, look at your life and all that you have created as a great mother to your own children. You learned to listen to your inner guidance and not choose to be like me totally. Children are only a gift for so many years. When you were babies I nurtured and loved you with tears. At times I was out of control as my actions were different from the other parents you knew. How do I try to make you understand I could not stop the show? I cannot imagine how wrong I had been. I had lost the time to change and to make a difference within.

How does one stop the reasons we do what we do? For me the answer is love. I believe that is all that is needed. I spend hours thinking. Then I began to live in these thoughts. My strength in life came from the dark spaces of my mind. My mind like everyones can be tricky at times and confuse even the smartest of people. I was troubled as you were growing up and becoming a young woman. Those were the years you needed me the most, yet I was not available. I was not capable of believing in myself. Children are like sponges as they learn. When confusion set in the awareness of my existence started to burn. It was my place as your mother to set an example. Your father was there to create for your brother the man's world or at least just a sample. I learned that babies grow up with minds of their own. Personalities and wants begin to surface when they are grown.

Today I am at a place of sorrow. The trees are all green, as people stand serene. The memories of life in the past make the dead last. I can see the stones, cold and silent, as names and dates are there to be read. It tells the world a little bit about the dead. Some are young, others so old, yet the silence is bold. The loved ones rest below while those who are living loose their glow. This place is not a pretty place but a quiet place. Sadness fills the air for all here do care. A park it seems to be, this open space with pain for all to see across their faces. Gathering together to visit someone in sorrow they cannot be undone. Society deems it that we need a place to remember a lost loved one. I always believed those who have died are still around but now in my heart. We are all given this capacity to love and share a painless life with others. Yet we shed tears of regret when someone we love is no longer. The ritual of visiting a cemetery with flowers and crying over a grave are for the dead, or are they for the living? Amanda, do not cry ever for me. Your love for me was the brightest beam that shone my way right into eternity.

Today you visited me and we argued a little bit about silly things. I saw the face of my baby and the years I missed because I was engulfed with the need to put your father above all. It was as if he had become a God figure to me. Yet you chose to still love me no matter the pain I must have caused you. I see the pain in your eyes and hear the sadness in your words. I have no words of my own to take away the hurt you are feeling. I do have my love today to give you but I fear in my heart this is not enough. I can't give you all the answers about life because I do not know them myself. I cannot understand your strength to crave more. I struggle on a daily basis to continue on myself. How do I change now to what you want me to be? For me the love you give in accepting me as me is all I need. As a woman of today, you seek deep down for your own beliefs and the strength, which I am not capable of. If I failed you, I can only say, "I wish love will be enough to get us through this life." There are many disappointments in life that one faces and at a given time they can hurt severely. You may not believe me now, but time heals all and the pain subsides to a place where we can choose to dwell on it or to simply put it away and go on. I want you to dig deep inside your heart and find a place to store your pain for a time when you can look at it more clearly. When you do release this pain from your life and move forward you will see how great your world will be. Age is your greatest asset and believe me fighting with your mother is minor to what lies ahead.

I have a few questions: Do all women change to become what they believe their husbands want them to be? Why does the single woman of my generation marry and erase her identity with her name change? I became enclosed in love that I didn't understand. I needed to escape to find a place and fill with grace. The inner workings of life I found to be everlasting. Could I withstand the outside halls? Was I capable of breaking down his walls? In my heart I believed I needed to stand my ground. My beliefs created that I was bound with a need to escape. I didn't know how to get out. Daily his angry words poured from his mouth. His ways were strong and his beliefs became mine. Although I never believed my own beliefs could be totally washed away. I lasted in his bubble of fear believing I had to stay. My life has been about the struggle. A long time ago before you were even born I was slipping away from the real me. I found a place I could escape to as I accepted his reasons for how I should be. I did not know how to be true to me.

I tremble as I read my own words today. I was scared for a long time I see. I was in awe of a man who abused me with words. Yet I continued to love him. Amanda, there is all kinds of abuse. Control and power over another is what your father was guilty of. You must remember that my generation believed that women had no say. When someone constantly knocks you down and then kicks you when you are in pain, somethings are bound to give. Through the years something kept me going until ... That is when I fell apart. I accepted abuse from your father but I could not accept betrayal. I was a victim in life to the mere belief that my indifference was created in childhood. I was capable of taking day after day in stride. I did not question and when I felt empty of love I ran.

The windows of my soul flew open today. Your comfort filled my mind all the way. To be able to share a few hours with you created need that for me was brand new. I look forward to these memories we share. After a lifetime alone, I found that you care. I believe strongly in the knowledge you give to me. An inner fear pushes me to survive that I now see.

I love my mother and today she has died without loving me back. I never knew of her demos and I realize today I need never know for they were hers. At one time, I felt abandoned, just left behind. My heart filled with sorrow for the pain in my mind. I was an adult with children of my own, trying to compensate for a mom who stood alone. For years my mind was confused, simply stopped in time. I wondered if all my life I've longed for a mom to call mine. I acknowledge my pain, my sorrow, and my hate. This I absorb as my fate. This pain I have carried for longer than life, as she abandoned me. Bravo mom, you never looked back on a daughter in need of your love for you chose not to see.

My daughter, my love, I remember a little girl full of smiles playing. Those years seemed to pass too quickly, now that I realize they are gone forever. A young woman with ideas of your own you have become. I'll always treasure the memories of you in my mind. I hope that your own memories can fill you with happiness for days gone by. So quickly children leave the playing behind. To be independent and strong are two qualities I lack. As a mom, responsibilities and chores were my life. A sweet smile, a simple willingness to be there for me is what you offered. It was a long time ago, since I had your freedom of youth. At your age I never had a mom to talk to. I filled you with fear through the years. Today I am grateful that you were able to believe in me.

I am filled always with the unanswered question of insanity that surrounds me. This fear fills my heart as daily it sits awaiting the start. I cringe at what has been. Shaking for the possibility I see. To tremble because of the unknown fills me with constant pain as I stumble and become insane. I struggled deeply and without belief that I was not true to myself. I know I was not on course with God's plan for me. Once we believe in God and fill with His love, He erases the fear and all there is becomes peaceful. It took me a long time to find the love within and in doing so I found peace and you.

I ask you today: Do any of us every really look at one another? Are we aware of the pain and sorrow of each other? Do we see or are we blind to one another? The society we call life are victims of themselves. Money, objects, and status are more important. The hardest and truest of feelings is love. To love one is to love all. At times I felt like a shooting star lost from its galaxy. I was struggling to see my own destiny. I believed I was a person filled with creativity. I just could not get your father to take the time to look at me. There was a time when I was deeply in love and filled with a bright light. Your father's wants and needs created an emptiness that filled me with fright. I was not to be a star in life simply twinkling in the night. A stillness surrounded me as I felt lost and in the dark with no insight. I wanted to scream at him to look at me and see all that I could be.

I let it show, the pain inside, and there was no comfort, no hug, as sorrow filled me up. My words once spoken could not explain the respect I lacked. My pain from within cried out as I began to shout that I must not be this way anymore. Oh, how he looked at me and screamed back, then slammed the door. I could not reach this man I loved. I could not understand why he did not care. He was my husband - he was supposed to care if I was afraid. He should care if I was scared. I needed him to comfort me in some manner. I started to really look at him then and I saw that he was filled with pain. He was guilty of not being honest and loving as he promised in our wedding vows. At times I let my confusion and pain show as I cried out for help. He was not capable of reaching out to me I learned.

I saw the hate in his eyes before that fatal night. He had left me a long time before I realized it was over. His words had been brutal for years as they attacked me. I was tired of his words and I had no trust, in his eyes for me I saw only disgust. I did not know what he wanted from me; after all I could not be anything else but me. His words would attack me like fists when I would rather have had a kiss, a tender moment, an embrace. Instead he would scowl and seem to hiss.

He was always guilty of ugly words as I think back. For some reason I really believed he didn't realize most of the time how his words could hurt. I wanted to help him find comfort from me but I was not able to. He was betraying me all along, this I now see, while I left the open space of life because the walls were closing in on me. I was troubled with dreams in the night. Awakening to find that pain filled my soul at first light. He was stifling me and I needed control of my own to take. I did not know how to make him not hate. He pulled away from me as I realized there was no tenderness. In reality I would have accepted a single caress.

I didn't know or understand what was expected of me at one time. I was controlled and expected to understand, to do it all, and still never get out of hand. The years passed us by and slowly he began to hate my sight.

Oh, the tears I have shed. I never was capable of speaking the words I could write on paper. The beauty I found in the written word. For me to be able to pour my heart out on a sheet of paper with a pen and feel release from the torments of my life helped me. At one time I felt that I should share my grief with others. Was I to be the only wife controlled by a man? Was I really alone as a beaten woman? I was not capable back then to let the words of fright out for he was capable with his strength of spinning me around and wearing me down. He lived his life his way. Only he knew his own capabilities. I was not responsible for the memories that flashed in my mind. I was filled with alarm by his actions that literally pierced my heart. The love I was capable of was solid like a wall. In the end when I felt I lacked the strength to believe in myself, I would fall.

I have to admit today that I was always searching for love: for the feeling of being loved. Did I suffocate him? Was that why he felt the need to betray me? The pain his betrayal caused I was never able to erase until I realized he had to live with what he did. Finally, I was able to forgive him with the knowledge that we are all responsible for ourselves and the choices we make. He was my man or so I like to think back then. As we grew up together children of a different era in time, life was good to us, as I look back in my prime. Silently I stood by his side so eager to please. Never one to make waves or create a moment I could seize. I simply stood behind him playing my role the best that I knew, always believing in him as my husband, with great value. I take the blame for the pedestal I put him on through the years. Never in my wildest dreams did I believe this would cause me to shed so many tears.

Today I have traveled to the mansions only to create questions. WHY? WHY? WHY? I never asked him any of these. I wonder what his answers would have been. Did you need warmth and love from another? Did you think it was love like no other? Did you in your heart think it was right? Did you believe you were secure enough in thinking I was not bright? Did you believe you were safe in your choices? Did you feel that I belonged to yesterday? Did you feel with her that you could be free? Did you wonder why you decided to stay with me? Did you think you would have to ever acknowledge your lie? Did you care if I would cry? Did you accept yourself for being like all the rest? Did you acknowledge that you are just a man who thinks he's the best?

As I am in my room, on my bed, sunglasses in place, I escape into a tangled mess of years over and over again. Searching for answers! Reliving the pain and crying in my sleep. His betrayal changed my world for I was in darkness. Once my eyes were opened what I saw filled me with sadness. I believed in our love as a special wonder. When my heart was shattered my head filled with thunder. This pain one feels at betrayal cannot be described. A battle begins within that erases the logical way of thinking, causing one to want to hide.

I found comfort, Amanda, in the beginning as I escaped to the mansions of my mind. I would silently lay in bed, alone in the dark as the sadness filled my head. I remember the pain inflicted on me, and the tears I needed to shed to set myself free. I would tremble as they fell, wetting my face, leaving a trace of the sorrow within. I cringe today at this memory of what I thought to be true. Once I realized that I was unable to start anew.

I looked back on my words from yesterday. How sad I let him abuse me this way. All I ever wanted was love and tenderness. Instead I withdrew into a world filled with emptiness. I stood quietly back, then waiting for his approval. Instead we lived a lie filled with betrayal. He found comfort in someone other than me. Finally, my eyes are open to a fool I now see. My soul cried out to me in my writing of the man he really was. I never grasped that he was capable of being the bad guy. My love was truly-madly-deeply which I bestowed on him. The power of love and belief can be given and also it can be taken away. I learned this a bit late in life.

Confusion was filling my soul wanting to set me free. I thought, could this be midlife for me? I no longer could see who I was anymore when I would look. Yet, a fire burned in my heart as if I were reading a story from a book. Loneliness surrounded me. This freedom I searched for was to be, once I looked inside of me.

Praying to God every night to rescue me brought the gift of patience into my soul. I await life's destiny in my heart. I await love to fill this life. I await your touch on my own. I wait for the time to talk. I wait for the chance to be by your side and walk. I await the knowledge of your love here before I go above.

Wondering about your mother? Who was this woman? Was she just madly in love, mentally ill, or simply crazy, bonkers all of her life? Trust me when I tell you that I was manic. I was depressed. To simply say that my heart burst would not be telling the truth. I was to be a victim all of my life. I loved deeply. I needed deeply. I hurt deeply. Like a wounded bird or a ravaged animal I cut off my own life to survive. I escaped to that place on earth where everyone is afraid of ending. I chose to live for years in a world beyond what is normal to the everyday person.

Love and dreams are what I am guilty of. Remember it's always about the little things, Amanda. I guess I simply could not get over the loss of another person in my life. "Loss" is what I would like to have put on my gravestone. The word loss means many things for me. To begin with I was able to experience the loss of life, the loss of love and the loss of time on earth.

Amanda, I was here on earth but yet I felt that I wasn't. I was the one who in living with loss was capable of learning through loss. My mind had taken over my existence and by finding that escape I was the one who was enlightened. When I experienced your love, my daughter, I simply couldn't take that little step back into the real world. One little step you're saying to yourself turned out to be a giant step for me. Savor the times we had together; so many people never get to share what we shared in a lifetime. As the woman I turned into and as the woman I had wanted to be I leave you these writings, a look into the mansions of my mind.

Well, here we are at the end. Yes, the end of my life. The end of my words! Do not fill with fear, my beautiful daughter. I will watch from above. I will place a tender hand on your shoulder when tomorrow's troubles grip your heart and you feel like it will burst. We traveled a long and tedious road together. I was lucky to have you at my side. Never forget in life there is a reason for everything that happens. If we wait and listen, the answers come. I was at a loss to comprehend living without love. The doctors tried to analyze me but in the end they were just doctors. Did they really care? No one ever really knows another. Only God knows us all.

The mind is a beautiful part of us that we cannot control when troubled. Whether I was sleeping or awake the fear would creep into my mind. I welcomed the blanket of fear as a comforter. I needed to be there and feel the pulse of yesterday forever beating. At times I will admit to you that the door would slide open for a moment, beckoning my freedom towards peace. I wonder now at those times why I chose to remain so committed and loyal to the mansions of my mind. The only answer I can come up with is that this was my path in life. As I followed and searched for love I was able to find a mother's love and a daughter's love intertwined for me in you. To say I love you, Amanda, is not just words. Remember that for me you were the exclamation point in my life! You are the strength and belief in the women of tomorrow. As you write your book, believe the one main ingredient in life is love. That is all God asks from any of us. I laugh today because it is such a simple concept. For some reason we do not know how to love! As your mother, believe me when I say that in the wisdom of life and behind the choices of doors we create for ourselves, all will be accomplished with love. Truly-madly-deeply, find your love that rests within. Dream of me, Amanda, and know that you are never alone.

I am grateful for the second chance God bestowed on me that day so long ago. I may have stumbled off the beaten path of my life but you held out your hand and drew me back to find my purpose and to connect with you. I thank you, Amanda, for choosing me as your mother to learn from so long ago.

Amanda couldn't tell if she was crying or laughing. In the silence of her house she is surrounded by words. Gracie's words and now Amanda's words joined together creating a book. Slowly she rises from her chair and feels calm at all that has been shown to her. An inner peace makes her see her own life's purpose.

She remembers times when Gracie introduced her to people as her "author." Gracie loved to tease her even going as far as calling her "mom" in the stores when they were shopping. Gracie loved to tell everyone that Amanda was writing a story about her life. She believed it was a very interesting life and would make a great book.

She marvels today at her ability to finally and truly see this gift from Gracie. How did Gracie know any of this? Gracie's writings were now able to encourage Amanda to believe in herself. For the life of her she could not understand how this woman, her mother, considered mentally ill by society, could write so beautifully. Gracie knew all along that Amanda was capable of writing a book. That this story would be about forgiveness, love, acceptance, compassion - because the path and purpose in life that we all are guilty of neglecting is the true gift.

Abuse whether mentally or physically has no place in life. We all become victims at one time or another during our lives as Amanda has learned from Gracie. How many troubled, lost women exist today, she asks herself. Gracie's gift to Amanda is the knowledge that we all are capable of loving one another. A simple act of love will make a believer.

- Chapter Eight -

Create

Amanda contemplates what she knows from deep within. She has devotedly cared for and unconditionally loved Gracie her entire life. It had always been her way to put the feelings and fears of others before herself. Today she had time for herself. Like Gracie had written in her gift to Amanda, she began to look for her own voice to surface. Through the years they had grown, as women who grow in friendship are capable of. Amanda was amazed that Gracie had such insight into life and the ability to live a life non-existing for herself. The similarities between both of them filled her with love and understanding. Gathering her thoughts she begins to write in her own words the meaning of life as she perceives it to be.

The words come quickly as I await the morning sun. To me this time is mine. To awaken – to write! I silently go downstairs into my library, as I wonder what hour it is in the darkness. The silence of the house is peaceful and starts my juices flowing. I enjoy my house the most when I can feel the silence around me and that is when I appreciate who I am. I need to begin as the words bump around each other in my mind all wanting to be heard. At this hour even the sun has not risen and I am still not fully awake myself. I know now that

I must continue on my journey of the written word. Dedicated, I am capable of escaping into the unknown, creating, dreaming up places and characters that pour from my fingers so fast that I stumble along, creating typos. I cannot keep up with my own thoughts.

I try to remember the time when I did not write or read. In the past my children always asked me: what did you do when you were a child? My face would light up with the memory of traveling to a faraway place: to sit and read a book. A game would surface as my own children grew through the years. Teasing me they would ask, "Mama, what are you reading now?" Through the years without realizing it I became a collector of books. I loved them all as I stored them away in boxes. I could not get rid of them. The simple act of curling up in any corner with a book delighted me. This love affair with books began when I was very young. I loved to read biographies and dream about these famous people. Always I was interested in what other people were able to accomplish. I became sad at times when their lives were filled with pain and torment. Joyful when the words I read were of love, friendship, and family.

A seed became planted in the pit of my stomach that began to grow, a desire, that one day I too would write. Daily I would write and store my words away, only because I had no belief in myself for as long as I could remember. It was an inner voice that in the past screamed at me that one needed to be educated and know about life to write about life. I became attached to my own words, for I did give birth to them. I was a silent child that would grow to be a silent woman as you have read. Silence was a blessing for me I now realize. I lived inside my mind creating my words. Always at work trying to compose the words I wanted to put down on paper.

Life moves on and days became weeks, then months, then years. I was no longer a child but now a wife. One day I became a mother. In the middle of my own life I lived through a tragedy that I never realized when Gracie tried to end her life. For it would bring me thirty years later back to my passion to be an author. It was my ability to accept all that was given to me and not to question "why?" This ability has enabled me to love and be the best I could. Gracie was my mother; it did not matter to me if she was sane or considered insane – she was my mother. In my mind a child must love their mother even if their mother is not capable of loving them back. I was able to understand her fears and her pain drew me closer to her. I was not capable of turning my back on someone I loved. Like Gracie I too am guilty of the ability to love – truly – madly – deeply!

I would turn towards the world of my written words because like an old friend they beckoned to me during painful times. In all reality books have always been my friend. My entire life I have had an affair with the written word. My love of books was part of the air I needed to live daily. Poetry entered my mind, fast, short, and heartfelt. The memory of poetry has always burned in my soul. Poems became a sort of tidal wave that flew from my mind whenever I was upset. What does one do with words that expose their inner thoughts for all to read?

The time to invest in myself was never to be. My heart pumped with fear at the thought of being exposed and rejected by others. I organized my poetry and stored myself away with them. I wrote short stories and essays only to forget about them once they were on the paper and filed away. A house had to be cleaned, clothes ironed, diapers changed, homework to do, and a mother to love. I forgot about the author burning inside.

Now it is more than thirty years later, as I sit and read the truth of my words, the joy and tears that they bring to my eyes. A lifetime in words that I wrote amazes me today just as much as Gracie's words that I have read. These words put forth my life, my feelings, my fears, and my accomplishments. At times it seems that I must be reading words written about me by someone else. I see on the paper before me that my heart was bleeding within. I shudder to imagine that through the written word I had created an escape and healing process to make me who I am today. My life has been recorded. My strength comes from my words.

Then I think of Gracie and her words. Are all women inside in their secret heart of hearts all the same? I ask myself. Of course we are. Whether we are sane or insane, young or old, in this country or across the ocean, we are all women searching for happiness. None of us are different in that aspect. What we make with our lives and our dreams can create a different type of lifestyle, for we are all created to be unique. Once you look within and find love that has been there all along just waiting to support and guide you is when the realization creates the thought: we are all the same. None of us are better than the other. We are all individuals searching for love and happiness to complete us.

I see myself through the years more than just a daughter, wife, mother, or friend. I am a woman with the desire to engulf those I love and need with all that they require to get them through the day. To love what one does is the answer to fulfillment. I love being me. It has dawned on me at this age that I have so much more to write about and so many books to read that I look forward to tomorrow like a child waiting for Christmas. The joy of knowing that there will be lots of written words to be read, as well as written, excites me.

I am witness to the belief that we are all capable of existing in life under any circumstances once we find love within and believe. Gracie taught me this by her existence. Through the years I existed on my ability to escape into books. Then when life filled me with difficult roads to cross I turned to the world of paper and pen. Once I saw that I was capable to find happiness from my own creations I saw the means of my own life.

To look back and be witness that all I accomplished was just the foundation for today has enlightened me. Gracie was right when she told me I would find my purpose and path in life. Like mother, like daughter, as they say. Well not exactly, except for the fact that we learned as we lived. We glowed with love once we welcomed it.

The ability to have patience and acceptance for another to simply be comforts me. This I am able to see today.

I believe that for me the written word has been the essence of my life. I have acquired a collection, which I see was created from my soul. In the past I did not need to be published for my words were the band-aids to heal myself. We are all just doing the best that we can by the choices we make on a daily basis.

Gracie has given me a look into myself by the words she left behind. I am proud she was my mother. I am filled with love for myself that I was capable to make a difference in her life. Thank you, God, for never letting me stray from her. Quietly I never questioned and this is the greatest of my traits. I never forced my own beliefs on another. I have been walking my path and purpose this lifetime since I was born; this I now appreciate as I manifest my dreams.

I have stumbled and picked myself up creating a life I am secure in. I have nourished my body and soul by creating words that will make a difference. The reality of my life is that I have Gracie to be grateful for. As my mother, she was also my teacher and she taught me so much without realizing how capable she was. I look at my own children and where the love for them came from was in reality Gracie. She was beyond wise and knowledgeable for me. I saw her as my mother and with that I loved her as a woman. I had no fear of her. I feared the outcome if she was in pain. I nourished her with all I had as if she were my child.

Respect is not for special people – it is for all people. Rich or poor, strong or weak, we as a society must love one another. I see people on the street and remember Gracie. They have her look on their face. They are lost and troubled but they are alive. Why do we as a society try to ignore them and push them in a corner as if they are not human? I have so many questions to ask. I wish Gracie were here today to ease my thoughts.

Gracie has been gone for a few years now but her words linger in my mind. In the end she never realized how she nourished me as her child. She was aware of my love, this I now know, and her memory brings me only laughter and joy. She was extremely enlightening for me. I look back on the years we shared and the stories we told one another. I will never ever forget her. No one can ever erase her from my heart. A mother's love nourishes us and fills us for our entire life.

I speak constantly of Gracie because I connected with her. A child needs only to connect with one parent as I have been witness to believe. Most fathers of yesterday as well as today go out to work and believe in their hearts that they cannot do what a mother does. Families become split with their chores in life as we are all aware. The chores of life could be shared and children would see an example of a loving relationship. This is only in the movies for many. The father works and brings home the money. He may mumble a word or two to his child, but is he aware of the needs of his child? The mother is the caregiver and nourishes daily the child from the moment one awakens until the night. Fathers provide the money and mothers provide the love. Can we try to change this in future generations?

What happens to the child that both parents work and they are left alone to fend for themselves? I see more and more mothers working today than ever before. I was blessed myself to be a stay-at-home mother and I believe that this is the constant that children need. It is like a foundation for them to always know their mother is waiting. It is the act of being present and teaching by this action that expresses the child is loved, unique, and important. We are a society who puts value on what is not important. Love is the important ingredient that nourishes all.

Chapter Nine

Realization

Amanda keeps reading Gracie's words over and over again searching for the comfort they offer her. Death is part of living, yet it hurts enormously, she tells herself. She was afraid she was not capable of telling Gracie's story and sharing with others that love is possible. As she writes she falls backwards in time and the world of Gracie. She would never be out of that world she realizes. It was part of her history, a part that filled her today with insight. She seemed to be almost in a dream state as she analyzed the world Gracie made for herself. An explanation poured forward of all that had been as a blanket inscribed with the word realization as a truth being revealed by another.

True love Gracie always had spoken of and how one is filled with this love and acceptance towards those they loved. To only see the good in people and accept any indifference from them was the definition of true love for Gracie. No one has the right to tell someone else what is right or wrong to do. We are all here to learn from one another. She can almost hear Gracie's voice whispering her story now.

In Gracie's mind she found true love for the first time with Rob. Her love was so deep that she believed she loved him more than her children. She became misled by her own belief. She fell off her path when she put Rob before her children. Confused, she believed he was her purpose in life. This in her mind was to love and be loved by him solely. She felt this feeling in her mind, her heart, and within her soul. It became her reason for living. As a child, when she was discarded by her own mom only to be left by her dad by an early death is when logic left her mind. There was no sense or pattern to follow. The children she knew were loved and had a mom and a dad. Their mom showered them with hugs and kisses. She hungered for a mom, for love, for family, ever since the day her mom had left her. Then Rob appeared like a "God" from the heavens above offering her his love. When he decided to take his love away the pain was unbearable for her to live through.

Her mind becomes jumbled and crazed to the point where she no longer wants to live. She forgets about her own daughter and son. In reality she too walks away from her children as her own mother had walked away from her. She accepted being mentally ill by society as the chance to live in the past. Those were the years that comforted her and she felt she finally belonged somewhere. She didn't count on her daughter loving her unconditionally. A surprise! A gift! Love for Gracie, finally.

After awhile Gracie herself begins to change and mellow revealing a person who may not really be mentally ill. At least her daughter doesn't accept this diagnosis. She sees a woman who needs love. With this love that her daughter offers to her, a bond begins to grow between them after years and years of Amanda waiting and accepting Gracie as she is. Together they learn about loving someone no matter what.

In the early part of Gracie's illness she is tortured by the pain and abuse her husband had inflicted on her through their marriage. She never saw this until she looked at her own writings, for she always believed in him. He was so above her in her mind that she accepted all that he gave to her. Of course, at one time there had been love and romance but when he stumbled and found others to love he began to abuse her and after awhile she began to become disillusioned. Who was this man she loved so deeply?

When she escapes into the mansions of her mind she acknowledges that we as people control our thoughts and our minds. She kept her thoughts to herself for no one need know what she was thinking, not even the doctors. Her thoughts kept her in the world of love and her memories as a wife. Everyone has the need to find safety within and this became Gracie's escape on a daily basis when she went into the mansions of her mind.

Slowly as the years pass and Amanda continues her visits, the real Gracie steps forward for she has the strength within to help those less fortunate than herself. She knows forgiveness and at times is wise in her approach towards her daughter. Accepting finally of the love she is offered, she finds in her daughter the ability to be the woman and mother her own mom could not be for her. The ironic life these two women share is a recurrence of the life Gracie shared with her mother. Look at the life they both accepted. They both started out in this world basically looking for love. Gracie searched for love her entire life or any resemblance that was possible from her mother that she could acknowledge as love. Her mother was not capable of giving to Gracie the love she craved. When she marries and finds what she calls true love a child is born from this love. Jealousy seeps in because Gracie does not know how to share love. Gracie does not know how to be a mother, yet her daughter is capable of being a mother and offering love to Gracie.

When Gracie's heart fills with an extreme amount of love for this daughter that refuses to walk away from her like everyone else, she finally accepts she is loved. She becomes aware and filled with clarity of life to encourage her daughter. In essence Gracie actually becomes a mom. This fulfills her and sets her free.

Gracie leaves her gift for Amanda so that Amanda now can create her own dream. When one accomplishes doing something they were born to do, they are able to find love. Gracie was born to be a mom to Amanda. When she accepted she was a capable mom that could guide and encourage her daughter even while institutionalized she found her true love. She pleaded with Amanda through her own words not to wait until tomorrow or when you have more time. Believe today in yourself and do that which makes you happy. Don't push your dreams away. It is never too late to live one's dream. It is possible for our dreams to be fulfilled. Many times Gracie had told Amanda that if she had been loved and lived a normal existence her life would have been entirely different but in the end she finally found what she had looked for her entire life.

Gracie's honesty with Amanda about life and living were her greatest attributes. She was capable when she chose to be aware and listen to Amanda and in doing so she saw that her daughter was hurting. She saw the light of goodness that surrounded Amanda and wanted her to look within. She wanted Amanda to find her passion. Yes, Gracie saw Amanda was capable of loving and giving of herself but what mattered to her was what she wanted Amanda to search for. Amanda was not as good as she believed in hiding behind her life. Yes, she was a great mother and loving wife but she too was being controlled by a man. Gracie had no money to offer and no gifts that she could possibly buy for Amanda. Yet she offered to her the greatest gift anyone can offer: a look within that all things are possible. She gave Amanda freedom with her gift to follow her passion. She wrote in her writings for Amanda to answer a few questions that would help her on her journey without her.

Honestly, Amanda, can you answer these questions? Who are you? What are your dreams? What are your fears? Is your life about you? If not, why? Have you become the person you want to be? If not, why? How has being married changed you? Was motherhood what you expected it to be? What is your greatest desire? Do you have any regrets? Look around at the life you are living now at this age. Imagine what you can still be and accomplish.

Life passes us by fast, my daughter, and I wonder if any one of us is aware of the changes that overtake the person from yesterday that was free at one time to dream. Knowledge is an awakening we have all lost but that which we need to search for to obtain guidance. Except for the lucky ones that are able to be true to themselves and live their dreams. The question that comes to my mind: how do those that are happy and successful create such abundance in their lives? My answer is that they believe in God and listen to the whispers of their soul, their passion, and that is how they live their lives.

Our story is about the relationship of two women who happen to be in this lifetime a mother and a daughter: love, acceptance, strength, belief, and support for one another. It is the love and strength we possess that shall create a belief that no matter what our life or existence at one time whether filled with love or without love we are able to accept when a change is needed. I cannot say that I am sorry today that I raised you as I believed from what I saw in my own generation. I cannot even imagine the abuse you were witness to that you accepted as the way of a woman in life today. All I can say to you is that I am proud you are my daughter and even more delighted that you will accomplish finding your own passion in life. We can all only live the life we can learn from.

Gracie believed that Amanda would learn that the true meaning of life was to trust that there is a process, to love and accept one another, and to believe in God. Gracie knew her life and struggles with the pain she felt was not caused by her solely. She was wise enough to know those she loved had to do their own thing. She accepted this into her life. She never judged those who like her were having a difficult time. She was not a silent woman or a fearful one that felt victimized. She learned how to live in this life with the life she was destined for. She had acceptance in her heart and forgiveness. She continued to love no matter the cost to her.

The journey she was on was to find love and embrace it for eternity. At times a bit twisted on her path by the mere value of life that a man can provide for her, she fell into the trap of denial of herself. In her poetry she calmed her fears about her husband by exposing his abuse even though he believed he was not so. He portrayed another face to the world.

She knew in her heart there are two kinds of abuse one can inflict on another. Physical and mental abuse is kept quiet in homes where it surfaces. At first she herself was not capable of comprehending the attacks on her by him. His words cut her like a knife in her heart. Her writings enabled her to pour her feelings out to find a reason for this cruelty. Through these writings she finds comfort and sees for herself how filled with fear her husband must be. The escapes to her mansions in her mind were a safety net for a time that she needed to rest and collect her need for insight. To hide in them was comforting for her during a difficult phase in her own journey.

Once Gracie realized that to get to the point where she can truly find love only by living this life with forgiveness, the windows of her soul opened. In reality Rob is not important to the path Gracie is on; he is just a stepping stone to her future. Once she sees the pain he is in Gracie is able to forgive him and accept him as part of her destiny. For Gracie knows that there is always a reason for everything. Without him Amanda would not have been possible, she rationalizes. Amanda is her connection and teacher who helps her to forgive, erase fear, and in the end brings her love.

Gracie imagines that Amanda will be terrified when she is no longer there for her. After all, she dedicated herself to Gracie for an entire lifetime. She will be witness in Gracie's writings that what goes on between husband and wife turns into a power game. Husbands and wives like to be abusive to one another in this society. She wishes she could leave volumes for Amanda but she knows inside of her there are volumes waiting to be written by Amanda. The tears will fall from Amanda's eyes but they will be for her loss and the sadness of this realization fills her heart. Her father was capable of causing pain and abusive language towards Gracie who he promised to always love. The hardest part will be to adjust to a life now without Gracie. Gracie knows in her heart the feeling of being without a mother. She was devastated by it but she wants Amanda to know and find that she is capable of life without her. To pursue and look for her dreams so that she can find peace. *This is a gift that Gracie wraps tightly with all the love she has for her so that Amanda begins to focus on her own desires. In the end it always comes down to free will and the choices we make during our life experience. Gracie's choices had led her to feel unconditional love, and this feeling for her was as well a lesson for Amanda to learn; she knew deep within her soul.*

In these writings Amanda learns the truth and how wise and sane Gracie was. All that they have experienced and shared brings Amanda to the point of questioning her own life. She rises and is amazed at what she has just written. The words all poured out of her as if she was a machine that simply was turned on and the realization of her life was to be displayed. Amazingly she smiles as if someone had been by her side writing and explaining all that is.

Chapter Ten

Peace

Amanda rubbed her eyes as she rested in her chair after her last entry. Closing her eyes she struggled to hold back the tears. Her body trembled as the words continued to fill her mind. Surrounded by Gracie's life and touched by her own story as well, she felt drained. Truly, madly, and deeply, she felt very blessed that she was the daughter of Gracie Jewel.

She looked around and realized she had papers everywhere. Slowly and quite stiffly she rose from her desk and tried to stretch. Looking through Gracie's pages she searched for the questions Gracie had asked her to answer. She could not for the life of her remember where she had put them. After looking for some time she found a stack of papers she had at one time separated from the rest for this was to be the last chapter of Gracie's story.

She realizes that all this has been possible for this is her true destiny which is in truth a relief. Yesterday is gone and today is what needs to be accomplished. All that she can accomplish today is her destiny for tomorrow. As she sits back down she knows she needs to finish their story that has been created by them and for them. She could feel her body calmly relax for she felt love for these words that poured from her heart. It was a sort of freedom for her to understand Gracie's and her beliefs were intertwined now as her own.

Gracie, she realized, had answered the questions herself that she had asked Amanda. Simply she had written her answers that today poured from Amanda to be included and to be shared with all that would one day read their words.

I am in essence of God, a Spiritual being having a human experience as I always felt God was with me. I am a woman that was once a child born into an existence to learn. I searched for years for answers while growing up. I took risks and different roads in life to find myself and the reason I was born. I became a wife after not ever accomplishing being a daughter. This was denied me on this journey. I struggled being a mother myself to eventually find a road to be able to absorb life through silence, patience, tolerance, and in the end unconditional love was mine to find. I was a person who lived, learned, and accepted all.

I had many dreams as a child growing up. I always believed it was possible for me to be someone special. That I see today is a strange thought only because we are all someone special when we are born, for we are all unique children of God. Growing up without a family of my own to love me, I felt that was the greatest and largest puzzle in my life that was missing. I loved all music and appreciated classical and percussion throughout my life. At one time I dreamed of being an artist as I picked up a paintbrush and paint but I had no encouragement, nor guidance. My greatest of dreams was to make a difference in life, to be remembered.

I lived a life full of fear only because I had no hope. I feared being alone the most and not connecting with someone. I believed that my life would end and I would be forgotten because there was no one to love me. I feared pain, and the loss of all those I loved was a constant nightmare for me. These were all of yesterday's fears because in the end the gift of love with the feeling of being love was mine to be after all.

My life was never about me. Being able to walk away from one's life is the hardest thing to do. I could not handle rejection and the pain that no one loved me at one time. So I chose to become a shell of a woman. I succumbed to the belief I needed to escape or I would not be able to exist and function in a life alone. Looking back on my life, I am witness to lessons I needed to learn, and learn them I did.

In the end I have become a person that felt loved by another and was able to love myself because of this. I succeeded in finding love after all. Amanda, darling beautiful Amanda, you know as I do that we are not ever alone. We walk with God by our side and learn all that He needs to see we are capable of. I needed beyond anything in my entire life to feel loved. To believe that I had made a difference in someone's life. I forgot my own dreams only because I needed to be able to exist this way to learn. The materialistic part of life was not important for me because I needed love to return to my belief in eternity.

My marriage was another story that disappointed me. I was capable of love even when it drove me mad. I truly, madly, and deeply loved your father. I never understood his growing detachment and disgust towards me. I was a person who believed all I read in books. I craved that fairy-tale existence. Amazingly married life was what I was never witnessed to myself. I had no map to follow or directions on where I was to go. I became a servant to a man that said he loved me. What else was I to do? I accepted his hateful words, never realizing he hated himself and not me. He was living a lie, which filled him with fear and pain to lash out at me. He was not honest and therefore he became miserable. I was not driven mad by him but by my own beliefs. I drove myself mad because I could not comprehend a life without love. The effects married life had on me in the end changed me so drastically that I escaped all of life.

Motherhood filled me with the ability to love my babies. Remember, Amanda, I never had a mom of my own to set the example. Being a mom is very difficult at times and one must be willing to be unselfish. I tried to create a family that I guess I saw on television or read in my books. It is very demanding being a wife and mother as well as being expected to willingly give up your existence and the life you had before children while still being abused by your husband. I became confused with the pain inside and I blamed your father's rejection of me on the children I needed to protect. I became like my own mother and walked away from motherhood, as well as being a wife. Do you see a pattern here, darling? I am proud to acknowledge that you were strong enough to follow your own path. My God, Amanda, your love is fulfilling me even now.

My greatest desire has always been the same since I can search inside my heart and see the hole created by lack of love. For me love meant life. I can laugh today because I did not live in life. I lived in my mind. I was safe in my mind. Now that I am no longer by your side, Amanda, look at the whole picture. Silently you will see the reasons, the lessons, and the love we truly shared.

Regrets are for those who believe they lived badly. I have no regrets because I fulfilled a void in my existence from the day I was born until even now in death as they say. I was loved. This is the main ingredient in life, Amanda. All the material objects we collect and need are left behind when one goes home to God. We can only take love with us to the heavens above. We all choose the lessons we want to learn on this journey of life experience by the parents we pick.

Amanda, as I am writing these questions for you to answer, I realized as I looked around at where I am at this age, do I dare question what I can be. I am many years older than you at this moment living in an institution and yet I own nothing. I have no money in the bank. I have no automobile, no home, and even my clothes are not mine. These are the facts of my life and today I accept them because of the one and only possession I ever needed. You! With the love you bestowed on me I will live on in eternity. Can you even imagine how happy I will be? It is a rarity to be able to understand any of this. Thank you, darling.

The love of a parent can torment a child or fill a child with the greatest of gifts. When children believe that they are unique and are able to fulfill their own dreams with support and encouragement, they become whole. I believe in a way, Amanda, that the tables turned on us, and your love, acceptance, support, and encouragement that you offered me was as if you were the parent and I the child. I am beyond grateful that you chose me to be your mother. How strong you had to be. I had to be a handful at times for you, yet you never faulted or denied me your love.

Amanda stopped, as the tears poured from her eyes. She had to be in menopause, she sighed, only because lately she cried so easily about everything on a daily basis. Her life had turned into one huge emotion. Blowing her nose and wiping her face she feels the tightness in her throat that has been there for such a long time. The life Gracie lived and the life she is living is sad. She is sad.

Gracie never knew what an amazing mother she had been. She was oblivious to her own great capabilities, Amanda thought. This was the last chapter and Amanda felt extremely emotional that with its end she would finally put Gracie to rest. Her mind would always be filled with the words of Gracie. Gracie had been the wisest of parents that Amanda ever met.

Ironically, Amanda realized that the education, which one learns in school, could never compare to the education of life that Gracie had given to her. Gracie had accepted her life because she believed it was God's will. Believing in God and escaping life for Gracie had labeled her as insane. Who are we to label anyone? Amanda thought to herself. Gracie's words filled her mind and she found them to be truthful and honest. She herself was aware of so many of her friends and family that had more personal belongings and collections bought by the money that was so important to them, compared to the nothingness of Gracie's life. She pictured them in her mind and saw what Gracie was talking about. They were unhealthy, angry, abusive, troubled, and fearful people. Most of them believed that true happiness was in the stuff they could buy and own. The more money they made, the more money they spent to acquire things that they didn't even need.

Amanda found herself amazed at how much insight she had been given by Gracie's gift to her. The love she felt for Gracie was overwhelming and extremely uplifting. No one would ever be able to take this enormous amount of love from within away from her. She found that now she too needed to honestly answer Gracie's questions. Her mind filled with ideas and questions of her own. She finally believed that she was not the only woman out there in life that struggles daily with all that is expected. However, she is one of the lucky ones because she had Gracie for her mom. She did see a pattern in life for women. Is it possible to open the eyes of other women and let them learn they are not alone? One life is no different than another. She was one in a generation of three women that learned from one another. To find the awareness and clarity that we can be of help to each other had been shown to her.

Her answers about her own life for her meant that she was accepting that life passes us all so fast that we forget to do what is important to us. She wondered now how we are not aware of the changes that slowly take the girl from yesterday who was filled with the freedom of dreams and erase her. For those who are struggling today in life she hopes they could be honest as they read this story and listen to their own answers within. Quietly listen and you will hear your soul's dreams from yesterday, Amanda wanted to scream. Gracie had thought about everything, including giving her answers, as a guide for Amanda to follow. Gracie believed the knowledge and love we all possess is within. Amanda saw that the answers she provides will be an awakening of what she has lost herself. She knew that many are able to be lucky enough to remain true to themselves as they walk their paths in life. Gracie had encouraged her to accept the life she was given, as she had. In learning this lesson of acceptance Amanda was able to be free from the belief that someone else knew what was good for her or that she would ever know what is good for another.

Amanda wrote with all the love she could muster up and was grateful and extremely thankful that she was the proud daughter of Gracie Jewel… I hope I can honestly answer the questions I have been given so that I will be able to fulfill a life that is worthy to share and encourage others in some way.

Who are you? A question I never asked myself! I know I was born a girl that has now grown into a woman. I was a daughter and sister who became a wife then a mother. This has been a pattern of life for most women of yesterday as we married young moving from our parents' home right into our husband's home. As a child I was filled with fear that scared me into silencing my beliefs and my own needs. I have been a loving, good person throughout my entire life. As an unselfish woman that has put one foot in front of the other always without questioning, I am here today. I simply accepted all I was told. Now with the guidance from Gracie I am able to see how true I have been to myself and my beliefs. In truth, at this time in my life I do not know who I am. Yes, I am all of the above but I feel that there is more to me now. I believe I have a divine inner source that is my strength, which is who I really am and shall always be. As I write this story I am starting to believe I am a co-creator with God as I create through the written word.

What are your dreams? There have been a few that I created as a child. My first love has always been to teach and spend time with children. I feel I am able to connect to them honestly. I love all children and respect them. Growing up and thriving on the written word, I needed to write. As all little girls do I dreamed of someday being a wife and mother. To nurture and nourish those I loved. I would say that today my dream is for peace and happiness to be the outcome for all. Still the silent dream within that makes me twinkle and fill with joy is the ability to be an author. Today I am accomplishing my dreams, for I have taught my children well, and you are reading my story. I am an author!

What are your fears? As far back as I can remember I feared death and any kind of loss and pain. As a mom I have feared the telephone call in the night that something has happened tragically to a child of mine. Today at this age in my life I have been able to erase the fears of yesterday by the simple belief Gracie gave to me. With love in your heart you find peace and God. My belief today is that I pray and ask that the Blessed Mother watch over those I love and that it be God's will that they are safe.

Is your life about you? If not, why? What woman today can honestly answer that their life is about them? I am a woman raised to believe I must care for my husband. I must silence my own needs and put the life of the child I created before myself. Gracie as my mother was the first person I truly loved and devoted myself to. It was Gracie who taught me how powerful and necessary the unconditional love of a mother is to a child growing up. My life has been full of knowledge that I have gained from all those I shared myself with. How is it ever possible for a woman to believe life is about her? In writing this story I have learned that my core and who I am is in actuality the choices I made by the parents I picked and the exact path at this moment I am on. In being true to myself and my passions at this age I can now say, yes, my life is about me and all those I love as well. Once a wife and mother, always a wife and mother. Life for all of us is helping and loving each other by sharing, giving, and receiving all that we have.

Have you become who you wanted to be? If not, why? Today I can answer "yes" only because of the insight Gracie has provided me in her life. I look back on my life and the dreams I dreamed and see the following answers. I wanted to work with children and I have been blessed with my own to nurture and love. As I have guided them in life I have also learned from them. I wanted to be a wife and a mother and I have been very good at accomplishing this. I'll admit that there was a time in my life when I believed I was no one. This was only because others could not accept I was happy being me and loving my home, family, and household chores. Yes, I lacked education and independence for I worked in the field of motherhood that creates and builds memories, not money. I am proud today that I was able to openly accept what I have been told my entire life. I feared to do for myself and fell into a pattern of the typical housewife and mom, which enlightened me with what was to be my priorities in life. Now that part of my life has changed drastically and I can fulfill my own passions in life with love.

How has being married changed you? In taking my husband's name on our wedding day, I created a new identity to go with it. Through the years I have succumbed to be the woman that silenced her voice so that those I loved could be heard. I wrapped myself up in a cocoon until now so that I could do what was needed for me to survive. I am no different than any other wife. Man believes he is superior to woman. It is the society we live in which allows men to control women. This has been handed down for generations. My marriage like others is dictated by the strength of my husband who demands as much from others as he demands from himself. Any man who lets his anger and fears rise to the surface violently erupts the ignorance inside to be heard. Confrontation for me was a fear that silenced me as a daughter and wife. Today I am in amazement that I now accept my husband as I did Gracie for he is one of my greatest teachers.

Was motherhood what you expected it to be? Motherhood for me has been my sanity. I enjoyed my children and played and loved them to the best of my ability. At times, when I was overwhelmed, I apologize now for any pain I caused them by not knowing how to act. I may have lashed out at them because of my own fears. I tried to always love them unconditionally and to spend time with each one on their own level. I accepted their individuality and encouraged them. I have listened and I have learned about life from them. These children I love dearly have been my reason for living. Because of them I have been able to dig deep inside myself and question my life. I could not have expected anything more than the love and hard work that has made me a proud mother of my beautiful children. I bestow on them the freedom to spread their own wings and fly, for I trust that God has a plan for them as well.

Do you have any regrets? At one time my biggest regret was that I had erased my inner being. I struggled with the reason I was not capable of writing continuously because I was uneducated. At times in my life I wish I had been a braver person and that I had nurtured myself alongside my family. Today I have been able to nourish my soul with knowledge I have gathered together through reading a vast array of books on life. I had priorities in life and knew the greatest requirement for success is patience. I had a job to perform and that was my sole reason on earth. As a mother and woman I took pride in this knowledge to do the best I could and still enjoy myself and be happy. I am delighted that I did such a great job and congratulate myself. I am at a crossroads now as I am witness to all that can be. I have the future to look to. My priority now is me.

Look around at your life today. Imagine what you can still be. I believe now that the foundation of my life has been the one constant that let me be dormant all of these years. There are reasons for everything and anything is possible! I am ready now to accomplish my own dreams. I crave knowledge from the written word, which has always been part of my life. Today I must enforce it as a priority. Through the absorption of the knowledge I learn I wish to be able to share and help others. I am growing and changing daily. Many topics are calling me to learn about them. I have finally been able to find my own love within and to grow with it. To learn that I no longer need to be silent, that I am as unique as the children I raised, enlightens me. Finally, I have something to say.

I have always been afraid to step forward to capture what I need because I grew up as a child of a manic-depressive. A label which those who say that they love me are quick to hang around my neck. Society labeled Gracie and she accepted what she was told but knew deep within she was much more. She was not her body. She was free. How many are capable of this enormous gift of acceptance?

I raised a family that is bonded to one another by the glue of love I bestowed on them. They all know what it is to be loved and that we have the ability of choice. They are devoted to their dreams. They are capable of functioning in a world pursuing what matters to them. As their mother that is the greatest gift I was able to give to them. I set them free to learn the rest on their own. They might stumble and fall but they will be able to get up and try again; this I taught them with all my love.

I am able to proudly state that I am someone very unique. My purpose and reason for being is to share with others that love is the only thing that matters in life. If only one person connects to Gracie's words and mine, then I have accomplished in making a believer.

The Passions of the Mind

Amanda was constantly thinking about her past and her life as she is living it today. Plans "A" and "B" are how Amanda now thought of her life experience. The change she was experiencing was like a path to a bridge that she was being led to. Once she arrives at this bridge she will walk across and the bridge will vanish, will be no more. One side of the bridge is her past (Plan "A") and she now is creating her tomorrow (Plan "B") which of course in her eyes is a complete transformation.

Her journey has led her to take paper and pen to create a story of two women who learned from one another. In essence she writes that two parts are being created in one book because this story unfolds the life Gracie experienced which she chose to help Amanda to fulfill her own dreams during this lifetime.

Awakening with no question to what she is being led to by the powers that be, Amanda is afraid but not fearful. She moves forward quickly because her soul has come alive and she hears the plea from within to transform and help others by writing about all she is learning.

Gracie's wisdom is her foundation and allows her to cross the bridge now and travel an unknown path that is exciting and informative. She almost feels as if she is being pulled forward on this journey to complete knowledge and an inner ability that this is her destiny.

From these pages on you, the reader, will be part of the transformation that Amanda experiences because the passions of her mind have brought her to realize her purpose. At times it may even feel as if you are reading another book. But the truth is, you are being witness to the belief that there is a better way to live your life when you trust and believe in God.

Amanda travels outside the box to find and create a life she must love and enjoy because she is, after all, Gracie's daughter. The path that offers itself has been written already as they say in the stars. In moving forward to a life that she always loved as an avid reader, Amanda finds in words from many spiritual teachers that which she has been looking for. She feels these teachers are the new Apostles on Earth and their purpose is to share information that Spirituality is what it is all about anyway.

As the reader, you will witness the disappearance of the bridge and know precisely when Amanda begins to live the life of her dreams in Plan "B." Her love for self, for mankind, and her passion for what she has been able to accept as her destiny create a vision in the mind of a new birth, a new person. The truth is that she is the same; only now she hears the voice of her soul.

Chapter Eleven

Beauty

Purity – Beauty – Wonder
As I look outside I feel no hunger
Contentment and peace are now mine
I am learning to feel divine
My fate to awaken reborn as me
All my nourishment exists on this path I see
As an inner joy is burning bright
I am no longer alone which fills me with insight

Amanda was emotional and filled with fear since the end of Gracie's life. After completing Gracie's story she felt a need to share the story within her as well. She believed that there was a reason that she had been able to write Making Believers, after all these years. It was as if the first part of the book was to be about her life and Gracie's and how they intertwined with the mansions of Gracie's mind. There was a passion within Amanda that was growing and taking form once she had committed to writing a book.

She began a search to find herself. With her mother gone, her children grown, she believed she was lost and empty. She had not planned for today. What was she to do now when she desired to be someone that needed to nourish and help others? Her whole life had been about these qualities she possessed. Today there was no one to fill her with the belief that she was indeed needed or had a purpose in life anymore.

She chose many different topics to read about and found that she was actually studying rather than just reading books while hoping to find answers. As she craved and devoured knowledge that she felt was missing she filled with an emptiness that she could not explain as her thoughts would drift to all the years that no longer existed. Her pain was unbearable for now she struggled to find a life with purpose. The reading of new books consumed her days and she began to learn and grasp that there is a better way to live. She realized that everyone carries pain inside which makes each one of us a bit stronger. We forget to love ourselves for who we are and who we aspire to be. She saw the beauty within people and realized that so many are not aware of their own capabilities.

Amanda began to write as if she were speaking to someone and telling what she was learning herself – she felt as if she was becoming a teacher finally. Unfortunately she was her only student. Her teachers were the authors of all the books that she was now reading that formed a basis of spirituality for her to follow. She was learning now to comfort her soul by her own positive thoughts and prayer so that she could feel complete and not dependent on another. Affirmations which Amanda had recently read about were simply her own thoughts. Daily positive declarations equaled her own thoughts, which were helping her to believe in herself. The knowledge Amanda was accumulating had surfaced from her need to fulfill her own life. She was witness herself to the years she existed caring for all those that needed her love and support. At this time in her life she needed a completion, a reason for being, and to share with others what she was learning.

Believing that she now had a beautiful soul inside this body that she lived in, she was able to appreciate herself as a woman more. Upon rising in the morning she studied her face in the mirror and liked what she saw. At one time she did not see her own beauty and felt she looked disgusting to herself and others. Disgusting is a harsh word but she actually felt ugly in the past because she believed the teachings of society and the criticism of her husband's words and those she loved. Today though the beauty inside was rising to the surface as she looked at her reflection. Smiling to herself she was proof that the light within was possible. Amanda would glance at her reflection and proudly say, "I love you, I approve of you, and I appreciate you," hundreds of times a day.

Amanda thanked Louise L. Hay for the book she had written, called You Can Heal Your Life. This book found its way into her life and opened another door for her to walk through. She began trying the suggestions in the book to change one thought at a time. She agreed to change her thoughts, to heal herself, which felt right to Amanda. Once she read the entire book, what she read made sense to her and she began to change her own thoughts by picking an affirmation and writing it 21 times a day until she believed what she thought about herself and life.

She needed to remain positive and secure in who she was at this time in her life. Believing in a strong philosophy in life and one that supports her in every way she wrote her positive thoughts daily to express her new way of thinking. She felt she needed them to help her learn her true path in life. Her life had changed drastically with the death of Gracie. Thirty years was a long time to nurture and love a parent on a weekly basis. Almost to the year her life as a mom also changed, for her own children grew and left her an empty nest to love. Life was teaching Amanda she was not alone and that she needed to trust it. Her desire and knowledge for the written word and all she could learn became a focal point.

Over time and ever since Gracie's death she saw enormous change within as she searched to believe in herself. Through the connecting of holistic behavior with her writing desire, she joined two passions in her life. In the end she hoped to see this marriage of the two passions give birth to a purpose that would lead her to expand the fruits of her knowledge by helping another and a collection of many beautiful books as well to be written by her.

Throughout the day being able to glance at herself in her rear-view mirror or just by passing a storefront, her face was calm, serene, and beautiful to her. She felt that the beauty was coming from within and rising to the surface for all to see and be witness to. Feeling beautiful she felt free of her past beliefs and looked forward to every day that was now creating what she will manifest tomorrow. She had patience and was aware that she had taken a walk across an invisible line that she never would be able to return to for she was forced by her inner current to move forward.

Amanda knew that for years she was not able to feel this way. She was a very busy daughter, wife, and mother. Enjoying her life in the past had an existence of living but not partaking of all that had been offered to her. She engulfed herself in the life of caring for others and making sure they were happy. She had somehow placed herself on a shelf back then. She did what she thought of as what was expected of her. These were not bad things but her behavior enabled her to choose a life that was silent. She lived and loved but not herself by choice.

Every day Amanda would journal as a look within to her own thoughts. Today I walked on the beach, she began to write, and felt the cold wind on my cheeks. All bundled up surrounded by crashing waves, wet sand, seagulls and birds as my companions, I felt alive. I was warmed by the glow of beauty on my healthy cheeks as I looked towards the sun to gather warmth into my being. My ego stepped aside for this was a moment for my soul to relish in. Gracie was everywhere I looked as tears filled my eyes, and I connected with the child of yesterday. Gracie's own stories of her treasured memories with her father on the beach so long ago just watching the waves crash flashed in my mind.

All children are beautiful and are always filled with love because it is within them to know no other way, she thought to herself. Memories of loving the beach as a child surfaced and asked me, "Where have you been?" I pondered the answer to this question as if I had been away it seemed from my own life. My soul thanked me for awakening from the silence of yesterday. As if welcoming me back I walked and drank in the beauty that surrounded me. Why had I erased this pleasure from my life I had no idea. I have to believe that to be on the beach today I had to live my life as I had, by stepping one foot in front of the other and knowing that there is a reason for everything. Yet, it was not my responsibility to question why. Not ever and I am proud to have always known this.

How does one separate the person they are, the person they will be, and become a person filled with fear? I have written of the years as a child growing up with a manic-depressive mother, a strong controlling husband and father, and the loves of my life, my children. I honestly do not believe I am any different than another woman. Isn't that what we choose to do when we marry and become parents? Society has drilled into us to remember our place. Very little is expected of women if they can clean a house and cook. As a woman who believed in the rules society set for many generations, I accepted without quarrel to do the best at the job offered of housewife and mother. I lived a life that was led by my ego. While my soul rested and waited. My destiny is unfolding now because I believe finally in myself.

I can think back on the years where my soul literally screamed out to me that I was beautiful. When one is filled with doubt which is caused by pain and feeling unloved they cannot feel also beautiful. This is impossible. Throughout my life there are moments that reflected who I was to be today. Back then I was not ready to let the beauty within surface. I was following my path, which has led me to witness the power of beauty from within that I shine with. The dark moments are no longer part of my existence. I have survived them and I am filled with love for myself. I may look the same but my soul is brighter and nourished. I was starving for years and never realized it.

As you read my words I want you to remember a moment when you felt truly beautiful. This feeling I speak of is a connection that we all share at one time. I pray for you to recreate a moment you felt loved and hold on to it. Remember that the answers to all questions are within. This beauty within that I speak of has always been. Life, struggle, and society exist as having all the answers to create the part of life we slip into. We have the need to erase the truth about ourselves. We become victims to what we think we should be, how we should act, and how we let others believe they know what is best for us. Abuse becomes part of marriage or even childhood, which we accept. The beauty within gets buried deeply. We are under the assumption that we have no say in our own lives. It is foolish of us to neglect our own heart's desires.

We are all traveling a road that we have chosen as our life. Born as a baby to our parents we are filled with the beauty of love, laughter, joy, and safety. Somewhere along this path we become filled with knowledge that drags us away from our own beliefs. We are learning daily from all that we experience. The choices we make are ours. There are no bad or good choices; we are all here to learn.

Search for the beauty within and find your reason for being here, today, at this moment.

I am learning that no one can go wrong if they listen to within. We are guided by what we as a unique individual believe. I am now witnessing the wonders of my own thoughts. I feel unique. I feel loved. For a very long time I felt ugly and unloved. I was not aware of this inner beauty I possessed. The detour I happened to take has completed a circle for me. I have tripped over myself, and in doing so I have returned to the girl within.

I read back on my poetry and shake my head in wonder that I needed to quiet my own brain, breathe, and listen. I see now back then my form of quieting myself was my poetry. I was not ready to attend to my needs for I was needed elsewhere. I was not ready to make any needed changes because I feared change. Like one of the stepping stones in life, my poetry helped me walk forward through my pain. Each poem for me has been a step to where I am today. Every day now I find I am filled with laughter. I actually find myself content with myself. I am that little girl from yesterday filled with the promise of tomorrow. I look around at all that I am capable of accomplishing with the knowledge that is falling at my feet so to speak. I no longer have any fear in my life, in my thoughts, in my writing. I welcome myself with open arms. I have learned that there is a time and space for everything I need to do. I am at peace. I cannot even begin to tell you how many times a day I recite this thought. In doing so, I erase the feeling of being overwhelmed.

I feel younger. I feel like I am glowing and bubbling over with joy. I am taking myself along this path to spend the rest of my days here with this body as my vehicle. I am being guided towards my future dreams that I dreamed yesterday. I feel very strongly that the ribbon of my life once tied correctly into a beautiful large bow will unite my reading knowledge and writing ability together. I know down deep inside that Gracie knew all along what I was capable of. All I need now to do is listen, learn, and pray for God's guidance to enlighten me. I have been practicing my positive thoughts daily and nightly, as well as writing and reading them. I feel my positivism and belief in change create the need for them at this time. I am learning my path is now about my needs, desires, and wants. I am learning that what is behind me makes me who I am today. As I learn that it is okay to have desires and wants that pertain only to me as a woman, I feel anything is possible. I have not exactly figured all of this out, but walking down my path to see the end result is turning out to be fun.

I simply can no longer get upset about things. I now have a different outlook and belief on life. I am filled literally with peace. I smile at myself constantly. I even find myself laughing at my image because I can see that I am definitely glowing. I feel great and I want to share my greatness with you. My new motto: "God's will is my will." I am so aware and tuned into people I feel their sadness at times fill me up. I wonder if I am to be a counselor for women who suffer in their own pain and lost worlds. Somehow I am destined to help those that turn to me. As I am learning so much about myself I come across myself in other women. For like me and my knowledge today that I was not true to myself for a very long time, others too are hurting from deep within. Memories pop into my head from yesterday to show me where I shut down because of fear. I allowed others to mentally abuse me believing that I had no say, when in reality I did have a say for I had a right to speak my truth.

I was raised by my parents that children are to be seen and not heard as the motto was written, and I believed this to my core and in doing so I withdrew from my own needs. Society does not teach us to believe in ourselves so we crumble at our own feet. We become overweight, we become ill, we become sad, critical, and angry filling up with fear because we believe we are not beautiful, unique, or special. Beauty is not in the eye of the beholder; beauty is within all of us. Don't let anybody tell you differently.

For years I felt I was in need of love and tenderness. I did not know how to obtain the feeling of being loved. I changed myself to get through the pain inflicted on me. I withdrew into books to comfort my soul. Today I believe that the written word was a form of therapy. The written word has been my blanket of warmth, covering and protecting my soul. I was not ready in the past to admit I was neglecting myself. I was very busy loving those around me and pushed myself aside. Today I am ready for me. Today I have no fear of tomorrow. Today I thank Gracie for leading me towards my purpose in this life by her simple belief that I could write. In reality I did not believe I could write.

I trust myself now by the thoughts that I am great. I allow myself to be that which completes me. I know today that no one can complete me; it is I that must complete me. As long as I can remember there were flickers of moments where I knew I was not being true to myself; then that is the meaning of my life. My own denials given to me by generations of women before me that I learned from. I always put others before me because I believed that I had to and in doing so I avoided confrontation. This is who I am. I never thought of it as I was neglecting my needs and wants. I believed always in tomorrow and that it was waiting for me. What did I know? What did I need? My answers were always that it didn't matter to me because I was not living a life for myself. Others needed me. I have been blessed always with the gift of sharing. In essence what I had to say was not important because I loved those who needed to be loved.

In the books I read today compared to yesterday I find the beauty to obtain knowledge from them. The difference is that yesterday I read to escape; today I read to learn. What is life really about if not about loving and caring for those you share your life with? By becoming a wife and then a mother at an early age I thrived with the world I was offered. I never questioned because I was having a good time. My beauty has always been that I am a strong woman who can protect her own.

If I could not today be able to handle the death of my mother, then I would believe I have been a victim and I have chosen to give up. Instead I turned to find answers about the life I shared with Gracie and the life I am to share with the world. I needed to find answers and why I felt unloved and lonely. I still crave the smell of clothes as I iron them, the little things like cutting up a tomato, cooking dinner, and even the smell of laundry detergent brightens my existence. I do not now or in the past have I ever shunned these acts. I thrived always on the caring and nurturing of my family. It was a pleasure I performed willingly and a way of expressing my love for them.

The part that swallowed me up and sank me into darkness was the dependence on my husband for money. I worked before I was married and while I was married before my children were born. The need for money was not desired for years. My husband provided all that I needed. When I turned fifty, realization hit that I had to ask my husband for money to buy anything for myself, and then I was questioned by him: why? How did I get to be this age and have no plan? This shook me to my roots.

- Chapter Twelve -

Faith

Love, compassion, and goodness lead one toward their faith
With the warmth obtained from all three one feels great
Realizing love is the brightest beam of light completely
Enlightens one with compassion in life to seek all that is quietly
Finally one feels forgiveness erase yesterday's dismay
As God's love washes away disbelief one is shown the way

L ove filled Amanda, and she was able to look at her life in a satisfactory manner. Once she realized that she had never really been truly alone and that God watched over her she felt a relief that Gracie had been her mother. She was forever thankful to Gracie after all these years that she was no longer silenced and able to share the knowledge inside herself with others through the written word. Gracie's belief in Amanda shone through her entire life. Looking back on their talks and years spent loving one another and accepting each other put a smile on Amanda's face. The word that was the brightest for Amanda was acceptance, for both of them simply accepted one another totally. Gracie knew all along of the outcome, and Amanda knew better today to question her belief. She silently filled her thoughts with loving memories of Gracie, the only person who loved her for herself. Ironically, they had taught one another about the true meaning of love one can experience.

For years Amanda felt that Gracie would die and go to hell because, after all, she tried to commit suicide. She knew there was a time that Gracie believed in God and that was why she accepted her life. After the burial Mass and the Priest talked as if he knew Gracie, Amanda believed that she was forgiven all her difficult choices. Gracie had learned the lessons in life that were required of her. This helped Amanda question her own life as well.

I believe in God, the Blessed Mother, Angels, Spirit Guides, Allah, and Buddha and that there is a Divine Intelligence greater than me. Whatever name you choose to call it, believe that there is only one Religion and that it is LOVE. Always, these beliefs have been mine. I was raised as a Catholic and felt special being one. I learned to pray and to attend Mass, as well as receiving the Sacraments of the Catholic faith. Like most of my generation I fell away from the Church when Latin was eliminated. The mystery of Latin made going to Church more sacred back then, at least for me. I remember for years the rituals of my religion and upbringing.

The time came when I no longer answered to the nuns and priests. I was in public high school and knew better than what I was taught in Catholic school. I would walk the avenue on Sundays and window-shop. Lie to my parents and then on Saturdays go to Confession and ask for forgiveness from the Priest and God. A few quick Hail Mary's, maybe an Our Father, and I would be forgiven, good as new.

The miracle of belief has a conscience and I was reminded when I strayed. After high school I would enter the world of work for a short time, then marriage was mine at an early age. I believed God was everywhere and not just in a building called Church. Why tell a Priest my sins when I could tell God them and ask Him directly to forgive me? I was afraid of this man called a Priest who I was told represented God. I feared talking to him. I was raised to believe that it was bad to sin. I never believed I was a bad girl as the nuns liked to drill into the children. Eventually I fell away from the beliefs I was raised with but mostly just eliminating Mass and Confession. I could throughout my life stop into Church anytime and light a candle, say a quick prayer, and feel I was still Catholic. This became my choice.

When my children were born I raised them as Catholic and to receive the Sacraments but if they did not attend Mass with their class then they did not attend. I believed my job was to set a good example. I was to love them individually and to guide them with this love unconditionally. While my soul slept through these years my ego grew stronger. I had the power of being a parent. They had to listen to me. I raised my children to know of God, but unlike me they had no fear of Him. My generation has the belief but we are filled with the fear of what we were taught. We knew of sin, heaven, hell, and the devil. To actually believe he was watching us and waiting to punish our sins. Today, I question: where did this belief ever stem from? This for me is frightening to write nevertheless to believe. How many times was I told as a child that God was watching me and He would punish me if I was bad? Better yet I would die and go to hell. Confusing me even more, I was told that God would forgive me my sins and all would be well. Could they not make up their minds? This confusion was topped with the world of devils, hell, and punishment which filled me with the fear of God.

Today I know that God is Love. He is the light of love and does not punish anyone. We punish ourselves when we do wrong. We carry regret, negativity, and guilt about our own actions and thoughts. We are the ones responsible for our own thoughts and beliefs. No one is capable of telling us what to think. Once we choose to think loving, happy, healthy thoughts we then live loving, happy, healthy lives filled with the love of God. This is the true miracle of believing.

In always believing in God, although at times fearful of Him, I realized I have never been alone. My ego however being part of me that was stronger because my soul was pushed to the back of my existence created fear in my life. This fear overwhelmed me into believing I was unloved. I was consumed for years with a building up of fear about life and living.

Let us gather together my beliefs of yesterday. I was ugly, filled with fear, and unloved. Today I am beautiful. I feel loved and fearless as I share my life with God. I have stumbled onto this path of change because I listened to the cries of my soul finally. My soul is growing stronger every day filling me with the miracle of belief. God has never forsaken me. He simply waited for me to welcome Him into my life. Once I turned to ask Him for guidance and for Him to gather me in His arms I learned of the miracle and strength of belief. God has shown me that all is possible; all we need to do is talk to Him. I am filled with the light of His love, which has released all of my fears.

God is the only one who has the power to help us. This is the miracle that I find to be the greatest accomplishment because I believe. Do you have any idea what it is to have no fear? No fear of another? No fear of any thing or any place? I am never alone for I walk with God as He holds and guides me through my life. I need not worry about anything for I believe today that I have to be creative to find happiness. In doing so, I will find love and contentment within myself. I need not have any fear. I leave it all up to Him. "God's will is my will." In the past my ability for creativity was my children and the joy they brought me. This is belief in what one is capable of.

My belief allows me today to know that He is guiding my hand as I write at this moment. He guides my speech I now see too. I am so positive that I am filled with the wonder of all that is surrounding me. To believe is more than a miracle; it is to finally see and recognize that there is a Divine Intelligence. Acceptance of God into our daily lives is a good thing, a positive way of living, and a satisfying existence.

I am light on my feet; my soul has wings as my breath cleanses my path. To learn that passion for love has been with me since the moment I was conceived comforts me. Today is a new day filled with love. Today is a new day to listen to within. Today is tomorrow filled with love.

No one takes time to cultivate their life. We walk away from the first sign of pain which we need to nurture for one another and listen to each other. If when troubled we turned to one another and remembered when love began and we believed in each other we would be saved. I believe as a society we never realize the strength we possess to love one another. Change scares people. We all find comfort being and doing the same thing over and over, day after day, for years. The world is vast and open for us to explore it but most importantly to love.

As a child growing up everyone needs to connect with another person in a good way, whether through the act of love or kindness I always believed. The child who has no one to connect to becomes lost and untrusting of life as they grow. They lack the encouragement to dream and be a child that feels loved. The pressures of life are given to them to face too early. Most of these people put an amount or total on how to achieve happiness and even love. In the end all they succeed in proving is that they have the power over others because they control the money. Money is of no use in heaven for anybody, as Gracie reminded me always. The child that is held the carrot of the dollar to perform and do well will suffer in life deeply because they will always need more. Children need encouragement, support, and guidance, not money, growing up. Everyone has to find some way to create for a child the true experience of feeling loved.

I find it amazing as I witness the slowing down process of my life. I truly believe I have found the key to success – believe in God. As a child I was filled with the wonder of God's love. I believed and prayed and was a good Catholic girl. Going to Catholic school and having nuns drill into me that God was watching kept me obedient and fearful.

The most important comfort for me at this time is when I feel God's arms hugging me at a difficult moment. The world is filled with hate, negativity, and people being mean to one another. If you truly believe in God and accept Him as your savior you stay in the peace of light He shares at all times with all. Like a new friend I know He is now accompanying me on my journey. I trust His choice in my path for the rest of my life to fulfill my dreams. I have many options for me and I await what will be revealed to me. To help the world and spread love through the written word may be all that is required of me.

I am grateful for my inner child screaming at me until I heard. I was lost and searching for something. I was reading about other religions, feeling desperate, alone and unloved for a very long time. Once the light from the Blessed Mother's love shone through, God stretched out His hands to me. I am forever in debt to them for rescuing me from despair.

Never would I believe that it is possible for me to find such peace and love from within. I have been given a gift to survive a lifetime. Once I decided to trust God with all my decisions, fear was no longer and I found peace. I was terrified when Gracie died because of not knowing how I would continue to live when all I needed to do was trust what I felt in my heart. I am witness to the good in life and all that can be accomplished. I feel now like a newborn child filled with wonder and love as I travel towards tomorrow excited for what will be.

At this time in my life I can read back on all my writings, poetry, essays, and stories to understand that I had been quietly on this path that is leading me forward into the arms of my purpose. I have succeeded in accomplishing all of the above without even leaving my home. I have escaped to a spiritual space. I HAVE RUN AWAY WITH GOD! I am in a place of wonder and knowledge, as well as nourishment, for the past year. God's helping hands has filled me with love for myself and peace that shall fill me forever and ever.

To be able to bring comfort to others because I am able to comfort and love myself is enlightenment. One of my lessons in life was to love myself. In succeeding I united with the beliefs of my soul. As I write about my life's lessons and hunger for love, I will be in the end able to complete this story which is very much needed in the world today, simply because everyone has forgotten that love is important to survival.

I set myself free by listening to God as belief in myself comforted me. To return to the knowledge that I am allowed to love myself makes me feel good. This then allows me to follow my path to creativity. I have been given permission I like to believe today that I am indeed a writer of words that others shall read.

I look at these prior years as a small stopover at a rest place. Now that I have refueled and nourished myself I can move forward. I believe inside I am different. I have learned all of this from yesterday. It is the beauty of insight that there are stages in life. We are born as babies, who grow to toddlers, then youngsters, teens, young adults, then adults finally. The time that is spent nourishing ourselves is eliminated. We strive to nourish and obtain monetary objects more than the comfort of our own being. We become victims of the beliefs of the people we travel through life with. My reason for being is to share and show with you to dig within and see what you can find.

The need for me to read and write is to spread what I am learning to others in need of finding their path towards believing. I am to be a guide through writing. I am enlightened and guided by a Divine Intelligence as to the words I shall write. Whether my guides, teachers, angels, the Blessed Mother, or God, they are accompanying me on this journey. I thank all of them.

"God's will is my will" is the greatest belief one can conquer. I am filled with the need to renew my life's beliefs, for as a renewed enlightened soul the beliefs of yesterday are to be extinguished. All those baby steps that I took forward to my place on earth today were necessary. To realize one's path and be able to work towards achievement is what life is about. I am at a time and place in this life where I must remember one thing as my priority. This is "Love." To believe, feel, and show love is major towards the future of my own well-being.

Foolish life and living that one exists in takes over replacing what truly matters. Material objects, power, money, and possessions replace love, trust, hope, compassion, and belief. Simply put, love is stronger than fear, the two choices that we are all given. I have learned that God is love, one choice; and that the ego is fear, another choice. It is harder to be strong and easier to be weak. These opposite choices in life are what make an enormous difference. We are given the power of decision to choose what matters in life to live productively. We all know that feeling in the pit of our stomach when we do not choose love. Yet, we make excuses for ourselves and take the easy way out. When we choose love we choose to be with peace and happiness daily.

The void in one's life is that little feeling that there is more of life for us if we fulfill our dreams. The dreams we create when we are young are the ones we need to learn to survive. The believer goes out in search of his dreams to fulfill them. He never gives up. The believer knows who he is and who he aspires to be. Filled with belief in oneself is the closest we can be to contentment in life.

Everyone's path in life is filled with obstacles of pain and joy by the choices we choose. To be a survivor of pain is to believe one has no control. We are all vessels at sea as God navigates our course. When we choose not to hear, not to abide, we are filling up with negativity and self-inflicted pain which is our lesson to learn. All that crosses one's path is a step towards their destiny. At times one is a teacher and other times a student. When we truly hurt and see no light is the greatest lesson learned. To believe one is in the light one can experience love and joy by being thankful for all that one achieves. One can be filled with pain that needs to be part of life and still be thankful because one is constantly learning.

Making someone believe is not easy. How do I explain that God has created me in His likeness? We have chosen a destiny before we were born is what I have learned. In life one must accomplish learning lessons to achieve this destiny. In reality one must listen and hear the choices they make. To believe is to hear. Once we hear we find love and our soul connects us with all the joy that is waiting for us. How do I know this? I do not know. I just go forward towards the light. This light is very bright and warms me. I experience feelings that are of bliss and contentment. I do know that I have had a strong pull towards books and writing my entire life. I know things that I never knew before by meditating. In some way by me choosing to believe, I stirred up emotions and knowledge inside of myself that have been dormant. Everyone's fate is their destiny.

This word, "believe," means what? That we can believe in ourselves and that we as a species are not alone. A greater, stronger, wiser force is with us at all times. Knowledge is not only in books but also inside of us by the many lifetimes we existed prior to this one. Everything we need to know we know. It was given to us the day we picked our path and life lessons, lifetime after lifetime.

For some people what is easy for them can be extremely hard for another. A child that can walk and speak before the age of one is acclaimed as being exceptional. The child that is late in accomplishing the same feats is considered slow. Why is not the slow child not slow but just moving at his own pace?

Children have all been grouped into categories which lead them to grow into adults that become set to believe only what they see and have been taught. This process we call life has no limit to which one can become. Whether the child talks and walks early or late does not differ in the outcome of their path. The child who grows to an adult filled with love and belief in which he is a kind person is the lucky one.

To fulfill one's dreams and live a creative life with purpose as well as love for oneself is a satisfying existence. To trust that another is guiding one is to believe. Everyone including myself has been guilty of saying, "I believe in God," many times in our lives. But, the moment that we trust in God, we become true believers.

How silly of us to ever think we are in control. Those who say, "God will punish you," have no belief because God does not have the time to punish or the reason to punish anyone. In actuality, we punish ourselves and blame God. To believe is more than just a feeling or realization that one is not alone. Love can only be given to a believer because it fills one's being totally. So much so that one feels and can visualize the pumping of love in their heart. Believing is a completion and acceptance from the lessons in life.

There are many people who say and believe they believe. They go to Church and occasionally pray when they need help in accomplishing a physically desired monetary need. Most of their days though are filled with abusive behavior towards others. These same people commit adultery, lie, steal, and are just deceitful in their actions. They are consumed by guilt and hate for themselves. They believe in themselves and not in God. Power is a force some need to feel over others. This power that makes them feel important is a lie within them forever. For the only power here is the power of love we receive when we believe.

Goodness and belief go together. When one chooses to live in the light of love and believe, all they are doing is following their path and purpose in life, then they can call themselves believers. We have been given a guide to follow. We call this guide the Ten Commandments. In essence, they are just to control the physical aspects of one's body and mind. For there is great temptation on our planet; these temptations of life are created by man's ego. We have run away with ourselves in thought and action. More of anything is better than less. Inflicting pain on ourselves and others is a quality we see as strength. To lie and steal is our ability to be better than another. To commit adultery is to prove to ourselves we are better and have power. Money is an essential part of the world we live in, so one who works seven days a week becomes richer. Our parents who have nurtured and loved us until they in turn need us are now disposed of to live in a community created by man because we are too busy. Our parents become nonessential to our lives. We are the important ones now and we are very busy.

Open any paper and death is portrayed. People – men, women, and children – are killing each other because it is their right to do so, they feel. Neighbors who for years were part of a family unit and helped one another now have become competition today as they struggle to out do one another. Gossiping has spread worldwide to the point that every magazine and paper is full of tales on famous people of today. We follow who they sleep with and who they lie to. It is very important for us to know how many cars they have and how expensive the houses they live in are, as well as the accumulation of clothes and jewelry that we must know about! This is called news. Man has been turned into believing that he is God. When one lives by these Commandments daily, weekly, monthly, and yearly, the soul becomes buried.

To willingly and knowingly inflict pain of any kind on another human being hurts you enormously. We are a society who refuses to acknowledge and feel this pain in our hearts. We believe in what we are doing when we are in a confrontation with another. This is our right to be heard and attack. It is easier to believe in pain than love. Men especially cannot show love because society has deemed this expression as a sign of weakness. In God's eyes this is the opposite. To show and express love for another is a great strength to possess. It allows your soul to heal and be nourished.

God creates miracles for those who truly believe. He is sharing our life at our side until we return home. He gives us choices and guidance along the way. To be fearful you cannot feel the goodness of life. Sometimes we must be at the end of our rope to cry out to Him for help and forgiveness. That is when you finally feel God's presence and love. It is like a miracle we suddenly feel but all it is really is belief. Of course, we are not alone. Why do we believe we are? Where did we all come from? Where are we all to go? God has created us to prove to Him we trust and believe that He exists and is waiting for us. With His love we can see everything that He wants us to see and hear.

To find this peace inside of us we need to believe that there is someone, a Divine Being, who has created us. No one in the medical field or scientific field can comprehend God's greatest miracle – LIFE! It is not our place to know. We are all unique individuals filled with an existence that eventually will fulfill and enlighten us. This is our goal in life. We feel we are accomplishing this goal when we are creating a healthy life filled with happiness and love. If we are performing in a capacity that we love daily whether we are rich or poor, that is the important key in finding our true purpose in life.

To put anything else before our own happiness is a painful daily experience. How do we find our purpose? We listen to our hearts not our heads. Our hearts are love and this love is our soul's capacity, once filled will guide us forward. Ask your friends and family if they are happy and filled with joy for the creative abilities they are performing daily. Those who answer "yes" are fulfilling their purpose now. For the ones who say "no" that they wish for another life, another chance, or if only they did this or that are struggling with themselves daily. They are not hearing the cries of their heart calling out to them. They are not listening to the whispers of their soul.

When we listen to our hearts and do what makes us creative and filled with love then we can become successful. Nothing else really matters. The truth needs to be known that it is much more important while we live to nourish our soul. To comfort and create a life that is filled with the only true gem it is and created with God as our savior – love.

"DO NOT JUDGE ANYONE" – words that came to me in a dream last night. A mere whisper that to succeed on my path, guidance I asked for – to simply be able to understand. To be one with God we must love all for who they are. We are not here on this planet to judge but to learn and help one another. A simple act of kindness towards another in need nourishes our soul while God smiles down on you while you take the time to stop and help another. We are all here for this only reason. To learn from one another all that we can. Not to judge each other believing that we know what is best.

Everyone is busy – rushed – stressed – faced with monetary values and this need to do it all. When another asks for help and one stops their life for this person one is truly God's child. Love is in all of us, deep inside waiting to ignite. When this light is ignited by the act of sharing love and only love, then joy and happiness can be part of your journey. A simple good deed can light the flame of love and one will feel its glow. Doing kind, nice things for one another is more important than hate, meanness, and unkind words. It matters what comes out of our mouths as we speak to one another as well as what our thoughts are. It makes a difference if we try to help someone in need. Trust me and grow into your reason for being.

We all know the feeling of accomplishing something for ourselves, the feeling of pride in a job well done. Imagine how great a feeling God will bestow on us when we help another in need. To not judge those for asking us but to accept an outstretched hand towards us willingly. The simple act of saying "yes, I can do this for you," places one in the realization it is possible to help another willingly with a smile on one's face.

Life is filled with these little tests we are sent. When you believe you know the feeling the word "no" can replace compared to "yes," then the choice is yours. The gleefulness of doing well fills you with love, compassion, and contentment. We are all guilty of forgetting there is time and space for all we need to do. We are given the ability to choose, which in the end makes an enormous feeling of belief in yourself possible. It definitely matters what and how we choose to live our lives.

The choices you make in life create the existence of love or fear. You cannot experience both. Either you are filled with love or you are not. To love ourselves first allows us to love others. To love others, no matter what, enables us to not judge them. In not judging them we accept them as themselves. To change from fear to love is a choice we can choose.

Life is a map which has many roads. Some are straight and some are curved and twisting. Within lay the choices that we are to make. We all know the right road to take yet at times we are drawn to the twisted road because there is a lesson you need to learn on that curve. Sometimes we learn and sometimes we refuse. When pain, fear, and despair are on the road we have taken we must try to learn what lesson it is we need to be taught and pay attention to. When we are scared and alone in essence we are not. We need to ask for help to let Him hear that we believe.

We are given sunny days to warm our souls and to get our attention. As we sunbathe, fish, swim, or walk in a park, just look up and beyond the sky and realize the warmth that is being bestowed on us. When the snow falls and our gloomy grey day is filled with the purity of its whiteness, this is a miracle. Hey, look up, remember He is calling out to us. We all marvel at ice and sleet and rain falling from the sky but this is just God watering the earth's garden. We forget to believe in these simple miracles when they are part of our lives all year long. We are given these miracles to get our attention to pay attention.

We have become a society that values the opposite of life. We have immersed our souls so deeply from the nourishment one needs to feel love that we cannot hear our souls cry out for help. Dig deep, look around at your life, and just pay attention to what stirs your heart. Whatever this feeling is take it and run with it as fast as you can. There are many choices daily. To love and be kind is the path towards happiness. When we choose this path over anything else we state we are believers. We are filled with dreams and desires to nourish our souls. If we disregard ourselves we erase love from our life.

People fall into the belief that they know everything. Only they can decide whether what is good for others. They can do no wrong. It is their way or no way. These people are projecting onto others this aspect of control and fear. When you believe you possess this power then your life will never open up to the kingdom of God unless you let God's will be your will. You will not fill with the promise of knowing your destiny. We need to just hear ourselves and listen to our hearts. The blinders need to be removed, for all things are possible for believers.

Those who put monetary value and objects as their most important achievement are wasting their time. Love for yourself and God is first before all else. God is love and peace. Cars, houses, jewelry, clothing, and money are to be secondary. To believe the accumulation of these belongings is of great importance is to choose the path of your ego. The path of love is the only choice acceptable. For those who cannot see this it is because they are still in the process of learning this lesson. Being that there are only two paths to life as we know of it we must all remember that this planet Earth is our giant classroom where we have come to learn many lessons. That is why in truth there is not one good or bad path but simply lessons that we must learn. As we become aware that we do have a choice it just speeds up the process when we believe in God and that God is love.

Chapter Thirteen

Forgiveness

The need to find peace in my life is strong
I know with this accomplished I shall be again born
In the end happiness will fill every day
As love completes my path I shall have my say
To share my knowledge with the world through books
For paper and pen has been my life as far back as I look
This divine inner source of my existence has led me here
To finally release this need of fear
With love comes peace followed by happiness
My need to accomplish forgiveness is my wisdom that leaves me
breathless

When I was a child growing up, Gracie always reminded me to turn the other cheek when hit or mistreated by another. Verbally or physically you should smile and forgive your attacker, she would tell me. A good Catholic only feels love and forgiveness towards an enemy.

I am guilty myself of lashing out and hating my enemy in the past. Through the pain of jealousy, hatred, or negativity I have known people who one day loved me then attacked me another. I never was able to understand this part of my life. I could not handle the anger of being loved and then thrown away as if I never existed. I knew in my heart that I did not do anything wrong yet they were now finished with me. My first reaction when being attacked is to attack back. I tried in vain to communicate with people that felt the need to attack me but never really being able to succeed. Then it dawned on me that I was not the one with the problem – it was them. The pain from others is what brings us love for them as well, I finally believed. It is my choice now with compassion and insight into another's pain for me to fill with love for them once I look beyond the face they show me.

In my own way and time I prayed for them and for me. One day I wrote their names on a piece of paper with an explanation of the pain I received from them. I felt sad that I had these enemies but I forgave them finally with the new insight I have been able to achieve. I threw the paper in the trash and ended the torment of always wondering what I did to them. Today I think of them with love and compassion in my heart. I pray for God to guide them and maybe help them through their reasons for not being able to accept me as I am. I have learned that how I perceive others is how I will allow them to treat me. If I just accept another and not take anything seriously because I do not know where they are coming from anyway, then their words and actions cannot cause me any pain. Sometimes I believed that maybe just maybe I did something to them in a past life and that they were holding on very tightly to the memory.

Ever since Gracie left my world and my days became empty of her existence my search began every day from the moment I woke up. I searched for myself and began to look for the dreams I dreamed yesterday. For answers and a life I could live with and be proud of by some way helping others with all that I was experiencing. I had received a tremendous gift in the papers Gracie left behind of her own struggles and demons she fought during her life. Just the belief that Gracie knew I was to be an author in this lifetime fills me with a deep love for her. She knew that this was to be my destiny once I began a search and believed I was able to accomplish my own dreams if I paid attention and asked for help in finding myself.

I am at a place now where I am joined daily with proof that all things are possible. I am so filled with this power that I have been able to forgive myself. After all, the past is over. Neither I nor you can change the past; we can only save today. I now look at life as being individual, which for me means that each and every one of us are to be responsible for ourselves. Still there is an invisibility that connects us all as one. After all, we all do want the same thing in the end: happiness. I am sure my own special enemies have their reasons and they know why they chose to inflict pain, sorrow, and hatred towards me. The beauty of my life is that I am able to accept this as their choice, not mine, and today I believe that they are hurting themselves more than they can ever hurt me. I have offered them my love and they have chosen for their own reasons to refuse me.

I have always tried to be a loving friend, child, and wife to all I share my life with. I myself believe life is about the mirror aspect which I have read about where we receive what we believe. The sky is a giant mirror and what you put out there is what you get back, just like when you look in a mirror. I am very conscious of my thoughts, words, and actions towards everyone.

My light may have dimmed for a few years but it was always there. I lost a great deal in my life through death and mental abuse but I never have been able to attack anyone first. My reactions at times in the past may have been the wrong choice prior to today but I was not aware I had an option. I willingly or consciously did not choose to hurt another. This is a tremendous difference in my belief today.

In learning to forgive I am stronger for it. I cannot be angry any longer at these people who in reality are mad at themselves. I may not know how to help them but I send my loving prayers out to them. If I think loving thoughts for them, they will feel loved: this I know as a fact. I am positive that God has shown me the power of forgiveness so that I would be able to write about the benefits from it.

Take a pen and a piece of paper at this moment, yourself. Write the names of those who have saddened and hurt you in the past. A short explanation of the pain they have bestowed on you. Fill your words with love and wish them happiness. Once and for all throw away these negative thoughts and forgive them with the power of love that is waiting for you. Throw away the list and be gone of this pain forever. Release the need to hold grievances towards anyone.

I promise you that you will have only happy memories to remember about them from now on. Once it is in your thoughts that these people would not be who they are if they did not act and speak as they have, you will be more accepting of them. I am a strong believer that actions speak louder than words. Once you throw that piece of paper away you are releasing them as your enemy. You are accepting them into your world because you know this is how they are and this is how it is to be. Only loving, kind, positive thoughts and feelings can lead you on to learning the lesson of forgiveness. God is with us always and we can feel His presence just by forgiving others.

The calmness and inner peace one experiences from love is amazing. Remember, we cannot accomplish two things at the same moment. To begin with you need to love, which will guide you to forgive. If we choose to hate, we cannot forgive. To carry the baggage of hate we then become hateful ourselves. In the end it is easier and lighter to love. With love there is no baggage.

The light of love will be part of your existence, which in turn fills you with the belief to wish well to others. Once again, if we are wishing all people love, we cannot hate, so we have no choice but to forgive. With the power of forgiveness that we now possess we then fill with only love. All we need is paper and pen and the words from within to release and forgive. Fill that piece of paper with all the love in your heart and then throw it away for good. Simply forgive what was and move forward.

You need never be negative or hateful towards others again. When you think of them, think loving, encouraging, accepting thoughts, for only you have the power to choose your thoughts. Our thoughts are simply words and beliefs that only we are able to think. No one can think for us.

Through the years with Gracie I learned to listen and hear. Our time together was long but fast as it passed too quickly. I was a very patient child, as well as woman, in my own lifetime. I followed my own inner guidance always. I was capable of putting others before myself my entire life. I am a strong believer that we need to listen to our inner voice. We let life override our own existence and detach us from ourselves. If we listen, our thoughts will tell us all that we need to know. I laugh today at myself that I was very accepting of Gracie and never tried to change, criticize, or abuse her. Still she was labeled by society as a crazy person and I never really saw her that way. That is the greatest example of unconditional love. Yes, I loved her because she was my mother but I also loved her as she was.

I forgive any pain ever received by me from another. I am clean of others' abusive words. At times I find myself startled when others speak hatefully. An insight into ugliness but in my heart I know they have much to learn. If I can encourage any change I'll share the love that is possible for everyone. It is another's fear that surfaces in different situations that create one to abuse another – that is all it is but their fear I now understand. In the past I took hateful words from another personally and fell down literally with the need to be silent and actually go to bed. The pain was unbearable yesterday because I chose to believe the words that lashed out at me. Today I have learned no one can hurt me or cause me any pain by the words or actions they choose.

I am not a psychic but I am intuitive and so are you. I am able today to pick up on pain and suffering that comes from dwelling in the past. Is it pride? Is it just their ego? Those who hold on to pain and hate, do they know why themselves? No! I believe they do not only because in reality we are hurting ourselves, yet we do not try to view others as hurting also. I have hated myself as I held on to the past and the pain inflicted on me. Until I saw that the one who is inflicting this pain is hurting as well. I then forgave myself first and everyone else. I look at them with compassion for they are in agony. I pray for them to learn how to release their past painful memories. The past is history. It is over. One must believe this and move on. Today, this moment is what is important.

Today I choose to smile, love, and comfort all. For tomorrow will give me the chance to start anew. Every day is a new beginning. I am filled with the belief that each day brings me closer to a life filled with God's love. I am thankful for all these words as they come from me to the paper. I believe in myself and this I now see is enabling me to share that change is possible for all. I was given this gift of creativity in the sense by just putting my pen to the paper.

In the past I refused to use this gift. Now I shall be honored to write. For the belief that I have found anyone can find as well. I ask myself, is it "new?" The answer I get back is "no," for I am capable to see today that God has been just waiting for me to ask for help and then I would receive all that I need to transform and become a better me. In doing so, I can never turn back. I am learning that once pain is forgiven it is actually erased for all eternity. I am feeling warmed by the words I took for granted at one time.

Simple words and phrases used on a daily basis. "Thank you, I love you, please" – all are words that have been extinguished in today's world. I am very conscious when I say these words and mean them. I am grateful, I feel love, and I know honesty is fruitful. With the use of these words you express more than politeness; you share respect for others and truth comes forth. How many times a day can you say these words and mean them? Every time you choose to recite any of the above you are given "a shot of energy that is stored inside your heart." Love is in our hearts. When we decide to demonstrate and show love in our actions and words we become healthy. Love is an ingredient that nourishes your soul. To love anyone or anything puts a smile on your face. In reality, all we need is love for each other to strive for goodness. Love costs us nothing but is very hard to come by. Once we are filled with this expensive gift we can be the happiest person on earth.

To love is to help others. To love is to give of yourself unconditionally. This is what I am learning in my heart today. I also know that I can only be me for my life is very important and I must make it as successful as it can be. Once we become aware fully that our actions, words, and thoughts come from our inner being we accept that there is a Divine Intelligence that is capable of lighting us up. There is no one that can turn out the lights once they are illuminated. I have found this to be impossible.

Today at this moment in my life I am sharing my existence with you. I have found my path to be the journey of sharing my life which I am to take. I am extremely proud to have the gift and honor to share as I learn. This gift I am being given is filling me with words of wisdom as a writer and a guide in the possibility of attaining the pure pleasure of love forever. My life is fully realized for me because I believe. My path and my dreams are all mine which are leading me to be creative. They can be no one else's. In creating them I create awareness and clarity which allow me to be fully loved. These beliefs center and ground me. I imagine you are wondering why I keep writing that my path and purpose in life is to be a writer and to share the knowledge by writing books. This is the miracle and wonder I have been able to realize. My foundation and love most of my life was the written word but I didn't believe I could be a writer. Can you understand and see how the tables have turned? Now I am being given the belief that, yes, I am a writer. I am a child of an alcoholic, mentally ill parent that was institutionalized for years; can this all be true today that I have grown to such amazing belief and trust in myself because I cried out for help? We all are the main character in our story as well as we all have a story to tell but we also have the choice and ability to write a new script for our story.

As a Catholic I was raised to believe in sins. Today I am aware that in reality sins do not exist. Only choices exist. The first choice we make is when we choose our parents. We need to learn from them that certain lesson that will show us the way to happiness and belief in who we are. It is never an accident who our parents are. Life comes easy to some because they are filled with love for all from the beginning. Those who struggle are in the learning process of life. We are a people that are given a life to benefit from by expanding who we are. Love and kindness come with forgiveness. Once we accomplish the truth that we can love ourselves, as well as our neighbors, we will be blessed with the gift of joy. Life as we know of it is just about the choices we make on a daily basis. If we choose to hate we are unhappy, angry, critical, and sad. Then on the other hand if we choose to love we are happy, joyful, kind, and compassionate.

To seek within our hearts to forgive is asking for love to be with us and to share this love with all. Compassion for others living on this planet comes from our heart. It is not felt in our head. Love and compassion together ignite tears of joy for one another. We need to forgive all no matter the pain inflicted towards another, once we realize we are inflicting pain on ourselves. Love and compassion erase this pain totally. We must remember that God simply is! He holds no grievances, hate, judgment, or criticism towards anyone.

We are capable of all grievances ourselves as we inflict pain and fear over and over again by our own choices.

We are a people who are on this planet we call Earth to love, nurture, and accept one another. This is what life is about. Man must help man. Once we choose to love our neighbor and nourish our family in a healthy, loving manner we are following our life's path to happiness. We will be blessed with the life we have chosen to live.

In reality we are here to please only God. He is aware of every thought and word and action each of us is capable of. He smiles within when He sees we love one another, respect one another, and are grateful and thankful. God has enormous patience and realizes that some need more time to learn the lesson of forgiveness. When we learn this part of our life's lesson we are on our path to happiness. We have the map inside of us; all we need to do is study it by becoming aware of the choices we make.

Chapter Fourteen

Awareness

We all need a daily moment to find our space
To support one silently waiting is God's grace
An accomplished moment of awareness in one's mind
Shall renew one's ability with the desire to be kind
As one begins to dwell in time that is one's own
One can fulfill their destiny if they believe in the unknown

W e all have this little voice in our heads and it most likely is called our conscience by many. As children we learn to listen to it. That is when we begin to either listen to ourselves or actually choose to ignore our own thoughts, pushing the thoughts we don't like further and further back in our mind.

As children growing up we all are aware of the child that is referred to as bad compared to the one who is good. Those children who are always referred to as being bad have a certain quality that surrounds them. The good child is usually in awe of the bad child. Their behavior and attitude are almost enticing and mysterious. Down deep lots of good children crave to be bad at least for a day. You choose very young whether to be a good child or a bad child. Those who decide to be attentive, aware, and responsible are filled with goodness. They live a life from the beginning always to be loving and good.

All children at one time or another grow up in a home atmosphere and become victims of their circumstances. Eventually adults that surround them daily teach them their own fears in life. Children are truly a gift and should be taken care of tenderly. Any sign of love and respect from an adult is absorbed totally throughout their entire life. Pain and fear and abuse create a different type of child. In reality then there is no bad child and no good child. All children are what they are taught and shown from the adults in their life. It always comes down to the choices you make.

When you grow up filled with the beauty of love then you can only choose to love. An inner light burns brightly inside of these children. This light never goes out. It is a constant companion comforting every decision for them for they have learned to trust life by the adults that shower them with love and acceptance. To love, listen, and choose to be attentive is to be aware.

How does one love? When we fill with calmness and beauty toward everyone, everything, all animals, plants, and objects, we find love. You are capable of loving everything. Look around and love something or someone today. Just saying "I love you" is not in truth experiencing love. Love is within and it guides you to do well, by accepting others by being kind and sincere. Sending a card for no reason, calling a friend you haven't spoken to, remembering to share is the basis of love.

How does one listen? This is the hardest to accomplish. Very few actually listen to another. We are very busy people. We have no time for anyone. Therefore, when people are talking our thoughts are elsewhere. We are so busy that we do not hear raindrops on a windowsill, birds singing in a tree, or the sound of wind blowing. The sounds of life are absorbed by the crashing sounds of everyday existence. We all need to learn to close our eyes and listen to the wonders of nature. Listen to whoever is speaking and hear what they are saying.

How does one choose to be attentive? If we love something or someone we must learn to listen so that we can become attentive. It is just like walking one step in front of the other. A pattern begins to form and an existence begins to blossom. We need to learn that there is enough time for all that we need to accomplish in life. We need to appreciate each other more and in doing so we will be attentive to each other's needs. Life is not just about us. Life is about living and sharing with others. A mom calls her daughter and she is fearful and scared; this can be heard if the mom is attentive. A child calls his father and he is distracted at a crucial time so he believes; this can leave the child feeling distraught. If you are attentive you can hear the pain and fear in another.

How does one become aware? To be aware is to be. In Zen you do one thing at a time to appreciate what you are actually doing. You do not drive a car, listen to the radio, talk on a cell phone, and drink a cup of coffee. I have seen many perform all of the above. What action are they aware of? To be aware you must concentrate on what you are doing at that moment in time. Try doing one thing and nothing else. See what happens if you just drive a car. No radio, cell phone, eating, or drinking. You will be shown the wonders of the universe. I promise you that. What can you achieve in life if you just stop and eat and perform no other action but enjoy the substance of food? We choose to be very busy people and we are getting ourselves busier every day with the modern technology that we are offered. Try shutting off your cell phone at lunch and just eat lunch. Imagine not doing more than one thing at a time and being able to survive. Yes, we are a growing universe with more electronics today than ever before but life is about living, not being plugged into a piece of equipment.

At one time there was life without the automobile, the television, and radio and imagine no cell phone or computer. Still people lived and functioned in a life that fulfilled their existence on this planet. Change and growth are good, but what must we give up to survive in this world today healthy? I have found the following to be true for myself. When I love I cannot hate. When I listen I am not deaf to others' feelings. When I am attentive to others I feel like I share their life. As I become aware daily of all that there is I am more knowledgeable.

In life we love so we listen, as we listen we become attentive which makes us aware. The beauty of life surrounds us daily and can only fill us with goodness. The combination of goodness stirred with love, listening, being attentive which becomes awareness is a very powerful existence. There can be no ugliness, hate, crime, pain, or fear in your life. You cannot feel well and then do badly to another. You choose these qualities early in life. With positive loving thoughts we become positive loving people.

As I visited Gracie through the years I learned to be aware of her feelings and the surroundings she adjusted to on her own. I never questioned her about her fears. I never put that thought into her head. I loved her because she was my mother but most importantly I loved her because she needed to be loved and I knew this. At one time I was terrified of visiting Gracie and seeing the mentally ill, troubled people she was surrounded with. I saw her eyes light up and fill with tears that she had me. I was never able to refuse her this small token of my love. I was aware of how she needed me to survive. I was capable of listening and hearing her when she spoke to me about life and her journey. She was a very aware and accepting person that I learned from. I may have had my own pain and an inner desire to accept her as she was but I never wanted her to be a different type of parent. I never imposed my beliefs or my needs on her. She carried an enormous pride in the life she lived and how she accepted the life she chose. She was not unaware of her surroundings she lived in; she simply learned to live and accept this as her life. She was a true leader in this world on how we can exist and live with only the need for love. That desire and belief was the most important part of her entire life.

I am traveling through many doors as they open for me where I can see I am not responsible for those in life who cannot be aware. I cannot be responsible for others' words or actions. Everyone needs to be responsible for their own lives. Gracie taught me this through the years. All I can do is to wish another well on his or her own journey in life. I am not nor are you capable of changing another with my energy and thoughts. All I would accomplish would be the loss of my own good energy. We need to follow in Gracie's footsteps and believe to "live and let live." I can share the knowledge I am given and you can choose if you believe as I do. I do not know what another's path in life is for I am only responsible for my own words and actions.

In reading The Seat of the Soul, by Gary Zukav, I am receiving answers to many questions. As I progress on my path to spirituality I am constantly changing and learning. I have learned about "five-sensory humans" and "multi-sensory humans."

To the "five-sensory personality," intuitive insights, or hunches, occur unpredictably and cannot be counted upon. In essence we are not aware of our own synchronicity or belief in ourselves, so we blow things away and do not pay attention to ourselves. To the "multi-sensory personality," intuitive insights are registrations within its consciousness of a loving guidance that is continually assisting and supporting its growth. To me this means that once love and spirituality enter a bond is formed that assists and supports the growth and direction you are to take.

Therefore, the "multi-sensory personality" strives to increase its awareness of this guidance. The first step to this is becoming aware of what you are feeling. Following your feelings will lead you to their source. Only through emotions can you encounter the force field of your own soul. That is the human passage in a word.

Today in our society the most common word has become "divorce." Everyone is searching for their soul mate it seems. I have read that everyone' s soul mate stays in heaven and guides us from above. When we die we then become reunited with our so-called soul mate. Another theory I have come across is that we are our soul mate. When you love yourself and accept yourself totally then and only then can another share your relationship because of the law of attraction that states that someone who also loves himself and accepts who he is will come into your life. A soul mate is someone who accepts and loves you as you are and to experience this love you must accept and love yourself as you are.

I have read that when two people marry, they participate in an energy dynamic in which they merge their lives in order to help each other survive physically. In other words, they need to love, honor, and support one another as husband and wife. Today the world lies and cheats on one another because they do not believe. In the end the majority divorced fill with hatred. They forget what brought them together in the first place. Their connection has been broken by lack of love so they believe. When all it comes down to is that their egos are stronger than their souls. We need to learn that head/ego overtakes at times the heart/soul. The head is louder than the heart at times. Everyone seems to only use their heads; very few listen to their hearts.

The underlying premise of a spiritual partnership is a sacred commitment between the partners to assist each other's spiritual growth. Partners who are both living a spiritual life recognize their equality. I myself have not been witness to many spiritual partners. The men in my life have all followed their heads/ego beliefs. How does one go about finding a spiritual partner? I would like to know. Spiritual partners are able to distinguish ego/head from soul/heart and therefore they are able to communicate. Their interactions are on a less emotionally bound ground than husbands and wives.

As a wife that has difficulty communicating with her husband I have learned that if I can change to believe in a spiritual life then why can't he join me there too? That ground does not exist within the consciousness of marriage. It exists only within the consciousness of spiritual partnership because spiritual partners are able to see clearly that there is indeed a deeper reason why they are together and that the reason has a great deal to do with the evolution of their souls.

Spiritual partners bond with an understanding that they are together because it is appropriate for their souls to grow together. All of the vows that a husband and wife can take cannot prevent the spiritual path from exploding through and breaking those vows if one spirit/soul must move on. It is appropriate for spiritual partners to remain together only as long as they grow together.

A husband and wife who are aware of each other in a spiritual way do not harm one another in any way. They are filled with love for themselves and for each other. Their paths are united as they grow to enlightenment for they are accepting totally of one another. The key word and lesson for me has been to accept my husband as he is finally. Every morning while I lie in bed I talk to God and ask Him to show me how to love this man and enjoy him as God does. It has made my life very joyous and happy to say these words every morning. I have changed my perception of my husband and in doing so his has changed of me. I feel that was one of our lessons in this lifetime to just accept each other as we are.

I am filled with awareness in every thought, word, and feeling. I am filled with love, happiness, joy, and compassion. I choose my words carefully. I am learning to think before I speak. I feel lit up like a

Christmas tree. I know today that all I need I receive from the Divine Intelligence that is. I am no longer alone, I am fearless. The gift of belief and trust are imbedded inside of me. I feel there is a beam of light above my head that I wear as my halo filled with all I can accomplish.

The power of prayer, with the power of belief, touched with the power of thought is creating miracles for me. To stop and listen to my heart/soul is comforting. I feel encircled with arms of love. I am protected and delighted with the beam of goodness and love that is filling me up.

A tremendous force calls to me to write. I who have written for the majority of my life have been given awareness into the ability I possess today. What I write today I never could have written yesterday. I am doing exactly what I should be doing at this exact moment in my life. This gift that I have been given is because of the choice I made to believe. My path is tying up all the loose ends. I can look back on books I have been reading these last few years as steps taken towards today. I have been drawn to certain books most of my life, and the bottom line is that they were all about information I would need for today. The simple fact that Gracie was my mother is the biggest of insights into what I am sharing with you now. I find that spiritually I am growing and taking charge of my existence.

I am aware at this time my writing is stemming from these "morning pages." What are "morning pages?" A book called The Artist's Way, a spiritual path to higher creativity, written by Julia Cameron is a 12-week course in discovering and recovering your creative self. The "morning pages" are three pages written every day of longhand. The "morning pages" have been the primary tool of my creative recovery, which has stirred up the dreams inside of me and in doing so I am bubbling over with ideas.

I am very happy at this time in my life as I bask in the glow of my creativity. I find I am so comforted by the inner belief of love for myself that surrounds me daily. I am filled with laughter and lightness of the heart. My soul is becoming stronger than my ego. I am actually interweaving myself as one who is filled with belief, love, and trust. My positive thoughts erase any negative beliefs that try to surface. The wonder of all of this is that I am aware of the changes within myself. I know when I am detouring from my life's path and lesson. I know now to stop, listen, and believe. I am here today for the reason of success as being a spiritual holistic being as I like to say in body, mind, and soul.

The wonder of these changes is that I am aware that I speak differently than I ever have in my entire life. My questions and fears from yesterday are extinguished. My guidance from books, especially The Seat of the Soul, has filled me with knowledge that has lifted me to another phase of my path. I am given answers, reasons, belief, and beauty wrapped in love from this book. I am so filled with love for my fellow man, child, woman, animal, and world that I feel my heart throbbing in my chest.

I also learned two new words, "spiritual psychology," which means a disciplined and systematic study of what is necessary to the health of the soul. It will identify behavior that operates in opposition to harmony and wholeness, in opposition to the energy of the soul. "Spiritual psychology" will bring to light those situations that could shatter the spirit if seen clearly, as well as support the choice to learn through wisdom. The choice to release patterns of negativity of doubt and fear that are no longer appropriate to who we are and what we are becoming. As I have seen it will make clear the relationship between the ego and the soul, the difference between them and how to recognize those differences. It will make explicit the effects of interactions between one's ego from the perspective of the impersonal energy dynamics that they set into motion, and it will show how these dynamics can be used to heal. I am extremely drawn to this knowledge. I am connecting the dots as I like to say. I am proof to the power of belief.

- Chapter Fifteen -

Fulfillment

The ability to grow inspires one with serenity
Enabling one the strength to succeed in a world of creativity
For one to achieve fulfillment is a desired ability
Enabling God's love in fills one with the greatest quality
Striving to become one in body, mind, and soul spiritually
One is encouraged to nurture oneself in God's image entirely
Finally to accomplish one's life path unafraid
One becomes witness to a detachment necessary to become brave

Today as I look back on yesterday and all that has happened in my life I realize I can never turn back the hands of time. I am filled with wonder at the lessons in life I have been able to learn to date. I, as an adult since the death of Gracie these past twelve years, have changed so drastically that I am proud to announce I am being fulfilled. It took me many years to get to where I am today but I am able to see that during those years my soul was preparing me for this change. I cannot really say I look back on yesterday truthfully. I do remember the major events in my life and the family gatherings we all lived through at one time or another. What I cannot remember or feel is the negativity part of yesterday. The ugly, painful feeling that dwelled inside and ate at me is no longer part of my life. I have no clue where the despair went off to.

This power of being fulfilled has erased for me the feelings from the past that were. My thoughts now are filled with love, joy, happiness, compassion, and wonder. I find myself skipping at the beach, singing out loud, and spinning around in joy at life. The girl from yesterday is filled with inner peace. This new feeling and attachment to nature that I have found was placed in storage throughout my adult life. Why, you are asking, and all I can say is that it became necessary for me to have the strength to care for an ill mother and not inflict my life on those whom I cherished. The way I lived and the belief that I was not important and that I was indeed not included in my own life was so that today I can live a life that fulfills me. I like to think that I was humble and accepting in the life I chose yesterday and that humility taught me that I was not important because I am as everyone is. I have found my truth and belief from my inner being and I am led today and every day by this belief.

For many years I was a mom with duties I never questioned or hated. I loved all that the label mom gave to me. My greatest love at times in my life was the act of ironing clothes, which no one ever believed was possible. The chores and demands of being a mom fulfilled me through those years. There were times I was sad or unhappy because of the pain inflicted on me by others but I never stopped listening to my inner intuition and beliefs about motherhood. I was capable of separating myself, if need be. My release has always been my gift which was bestowed on me ever since I can remember and that was the written word. Poetry came easy for me which I pushed away at one time because I believed I was not good enough. I feared myself because I listened to my ego at those times. The reality of life I have learned is that it is not meant to be difficult. Why do we as a people believe we are not worth anything if we do not struggle? My entire existence has been the creation of the written word as my foundation as I am led to be witness to today.

I have cleaned up the floor and can see where I am walking finally. I am being guided towards that which will fulfill me. This destiny I must remind you again is the book you are holding in your hands at this moment as you are reading my words. Slowly I can recall the comfort in my heart and soul that I acquired my entire life as I read or wrote. These inner needs for me to travel and escape into many books ever since I was a little girl have been my silence and at the same time my strength. I have craved recognition as a published author as long as I can remember. Life for me at times was very busy with my children to care for and a house to clean. I would write, submit, be rejected, and then stop writing and submitting sometimes for years. I formed a pattern of disbelief about my own capabilities.

Death of a loved one always creates drama and painful poetry for me. Being that I was an avid reader I read all that I could find about the other side of life. The author George Anderson became a close friend of mine as I read his books searching for information and answers. Sylvia Brown became another favorite. I felt though that something was missing and that I needed to be somewhere or doing something to better my existence. That is when I met the author Caroline Myss and read her book Sacred Contracts and learned about the need to soul search.

By delving into the world of a lifestyle that would be holistic and spiritual I fulfilled my power and wonder at life. I read many books on nutrition and changed my eating habits. I checked out the world of prayer, meditation, reiki, and massage. As a child I walked everywhere I needed to go and today I find myself walking once again through the streets of my neighborhood and at times at the beach. Then I purchased Louise L. Hays' book You Can Heal Your Life and learned the power of positive thought which she calls affirmations. I read the Seat of the Soul by Gary Zukav and learned about personality and soul work as I have written. The constant belief and love for myself has enabled me to receive and learn that the power of being fulfilled is a true wonder in life. I am in need of nothing as I learn that I am in want of no physical objects for I love myself and I love my life as it is today.

"To the mind that is still the whole universe surrenders," by Tao Te Ching; to quiet one's mind seems to be a difficult task to acquire I have learned. I found that when I visualize the ocean and breathe in when the wave crashes and breathe out when the water recedes I am able to calm my thoughts long enough to create stillness in my mind. This picture of the ocean comforts me for I am drawn to water. Recently I was able to learn that the beauty of nature is quite comforting as it reminds me that there is another presence in our lives.

A favorite quote of mine has become: "I close my eyes to see." How foolish I had been in the past to not remember to do this. I let life dictate to me as I filled up daily with fear and things that were not important. So many sights in my life I took for granted. The images of a life that we simply accept on a daily basis we ignore and never think about. To see is one of our gifts from God and to see when our eyes are closed is a way of finding what is important.

I have experienced that which I call detachment. It is a new word for me and I associate it with the word fulfillment. The anger within that I carried enabling me to go within and ignore myself has disappeared. My voice is mine and though in a sense I continue to be silent no one can make me raise my voice. No one has the ability to tell me what I should do for I only answer to God. I have learned about the existence of my own dreams that I need to accomplish. This is an inner belief that fills me with inner peace as I learn daily what is expected of me. "To be in a moment that I can feel and adhere to will satisfy my need to be me. For years I found myself locked up and needing to be free. Finally, God released me with His key. I never realized a simple positive thought regarding myself was all that was required of me." How wonderful to be able today to believe in myself. In doing so, I have found my way.

I am no longer exhausted or fearful because of my thoughts. Today I try extremely hard to have only positive thoughts, words, and beliefs to live by. These thoughts start with the love of all that can be possible, for mankind and me. I no longer need to know all. God knows all and that is good enough for me. In life one finds him/herself needing to know the answer to everything, why-why-why? I have erased this from my mind for I found that I no longer needed to know why everything is happening to me. As I am now able to create a world that matters to me for I am free to be me, I would like to encourage others to be themselves.

The changes I have chosen to make have enabled me to look back on my life and learn from all that I shared life with. By detaching myself from people now enables me to obtain fulfillment and I learned to believe this to be a needed choice. The need to express myself by words that show I am right, I have the answer, has disappeared. Why do we believe we need to confront another and argue and fight over silly nonsense? When all we need to create peace and love in our lives is to express understanding and compassion for others in pain. Walk away from fear and pain, just express love and peace in return. Change for me is total. There are to be no exceptions. I fight with no one. I am at peace. I believe in the process of life. I am free of yesterday's fear of the unknown because I am protected today by the inner ability to find the love within myself and grasp hold of it forever. The greatest joy and feeling that comforts me is that I am no longer alone.

Daily I awaken and fill with love for the life I have. I am grateful and thankful to God for giving me my parents, my husband, children, grandchildren, family, and friends. I adore the place I am at now. I write in my journal and then I meditate. I eat healthy foods and I smile at my reflection constantly which delights me. Remember, there was a time when I did not like what I saw in the mirror. I am writing today because I have this belief that we can all be fulfilled and love ourselves. This is the main ingredient in life, and I am proof that anyone can change.

I am actually living the second part of my life on this planet by returning to the girl I had been a long time ago. Life, a manic-depressive parent, controlling relationships, low self-esteem, fear, and belief that I was beneath others led me to look for answers. I have found the answers within and now I am being fulfilled. All that fulfills me today is the belief that I choose my thoughts, my words, and my actions daily.

Since the year 2003, I have focused on this change from within. I have read many, many books mostly from Hay House authors, and I think of them all as my spiritual teachers and guides now. It is amazing how I changed those around me by simply changing how I perceived myself. I have been enjoying my life today because I believe in all that is unknown by the human eye. I truly believe!

Chapter Sixteen

Insight

I thank God today in an Artist Prayer
For the gift of insight into my creativity
I am blessed with this knowledge
He has been able to give to me
As I become nourished by His love to be free
I am forever grateful
For these words to express myself to Thee

I had written in my journal that today I am able to listen and hear my soul. I then proceeded to look up the word "insight." The meaning verifies my own words for me. The definition of insight: sight into; thorough knowledge; discernment; penetration. I then asked myself, what does this mean to me? As I have journeyed forward to find peace and love I found more than one can imagine. Insight for me is to finally know that I am knowledgeable as I look within. To be able to listen and hear one's own soul is beautiful to experience.

I am filled with calmness that in the past escaped me. I have this new feeling I call "love within." As this knowledge that I am gathering through reading and nourishing my body, mind, and soul from within is quite wonderful, I cannot grasp how I felt prior to gaining this insight. For I have fled quickly forward to this space that needed to be filled.

I have come to realize just by being the age I am and the necessary changes of my body that I am experiencing all that is necessary to achieve a major change for not only my body but also my soul and mind. I see and hear goodness in the world around me. The cycles of life and episodes every woman goes through are basically the same. From puberty to becoming a woman by one's menstruation and those of us who become mothers and finally the age I am at now, these feelings are not unique but part of life for all women. In the books I have read about the midlife crises we all go through they forget to tell you that what they consider "the change" is in reality insight into who we are. Most of us choose not to pay attention and just fall into the belief we are getting old and all of these feelings are part of the territory. The desire at this age to learn and accomplish more with what is left in the remaining years has given me an insight into belief of myself.

As I am capable in acknowledging this insight, within a light is illuminated. Wow! I simply think positive thoughts and they are accomplished. I feel good and fulfilled as I nourish myself. I ask God daily, "What do I need to know?" The answers come to me. You're shaking your head and filling with doubt. We are all capable of what I am capable of. We choose to clog our bodies with the wrong foods, chemicals, and negative thoughts. We choose to not want to hear what our own bodies tell us. We are not ever taught of the gifts we possess within.

Close your eyes and breathe in and breathe out through your nose. Say the word "in" when you breathe in, then the word "out" when you breathe out. Fill yourself with love for everyone and everything. Feel the calmness and peace as it descends all around you. Learn to listen for guidance. We are all capable of this ability I call insight. Think positive thoughts as often as possible. Positively, I can tell you your life will change. The wonder of it is to believe in it and then ask a simple question and be amazed when the answer arrives. Read about 15 minutes a day a book on spirituality, preferably in the morning to set your intention for the day.

When I struggled on certain days in the past with Gracie's manic-depressive outbreaks I had insight into her need of me. I could have walked away from her like everyone else she loved but I was not capable of doing so. I believe today as I look back on her life and mine that we needed to learn from each other. In her own words to me she believed the same. In the past I was not aware of this word insight. I just believed I needed to do that which made me happy to do. I did it and I am grateful today that I was that person. All I am today is because of my thoughts, actions, and words from yesterday. I have learned an enormous amount of wisdom from all that I have met in my entire life. There is a reason for everything even if we are not shown what that reason is. We need to all trust that there is a process to life.

Now that I hear and see that my dreams function first as a thought and then a possibility I have learned to listen intently. I am so engulfed in my journey that I want to run forward to get there quicker. Through the diligence of patience and prayer I will slowly glide towards the future. I have begun a new life as I write, read, and learn to express my desires; I am fulfilling my needs. The beauty of knowledge is to hear the voice within whether it is loud or as a whisper. Insight and the ability to hear is to listen, for once we are aware and filled with clarity there is no fear, only love. When you hear a loud voice from within know and trust that it is your ego screaming at you, for God always whispers.

The foundation of my life is the knowledge I obtain from the books as a reader. This ability and the love for poetry has placed me here today on a path to write and encourage love, positive thoughts, and change. I believe that I am to share with all these experiences I am creating because I am living proof that change is possible. I feel at times that change is not the right word but that the process allows me to become a better me and that is what it is all about in the end. By becoming a better person in this life experience by sharing and helping another I am able to be a bearer of the light I carry from within. I can see in myself that as I read more on Spirituality I am beckoned to make the changes in my own life. I have been able to learn that my whole existence here on this planet is now explained to me. I feel complete with the insight I am given. There is so much for me to learn and I shall strive to obtain all that I can.

My life is filled with this awareness of the knowledge that is needed to nourish my soul. My ego is quietly listening to this soul of mine. For fifty years I lived by my ego. Today I live by the guidance of my soul. At first I was overwhelmed by this feeling that I had a soul that I could hear. Now I am more blended and at times my ego still likes to be heard but it is not as strong. I look at life in the form of Plan "A" as yesterday and today I travel through Plan "B." It is awesome to be given a chance to change and to grasp hold of it and succeed. I ask and look around at people and wonder, why can't they feel as I do? Why could I not feel this way and know what I know today when Gracie was alive? Simply, the time was not right

for me is the answer I receive. Baby steps are what life is about...
one step at a time.

I have lots going on in my mind. It is my thoughts that make me
today look at the world with an open eye. My hearing has improved
as I learn about my potential to listen. In the past I was never aware
that I was allowed to ask or desire anything. To finally trust and
believe in myself has made me feel strong, something which I never
felt before. To become a positive-thinking person filled with this
need to help others and share what I am learning has finally begun
to let me settle down.

My first reaction at first was that I wanted everyone to experience
the love that was filling me up and consuming me. Of course I
quickly learned this was not possible. After all I am the one doing
all of the work and being enlightened. I was distraught and searched
for answers and needed to find peace and love in my life for many
years before as well as after Gracie's death. As the one to discover
this change I had waiting within myself, I began to choose to learn
and nourish myself with the insight I was given. One step after
another will show me how I am to share this newfound belief and
love. In doing that which I needed to accomplish I found answers.
Understanding today that Gracie and I both lived in the mansions of
our minds because we filled with pain and let others lead us through
our own existence. When I began this book it was only going to be
about Gracie but I stirred up the passions of my own mind when
I realized I had a soul that needed to be nourished. The greatest
passion I have uncovered is that I have a purpose. In learning that I
have choice today I can only be me.

Amazingly I smile as I realize that I have traveled this far, and
not knowing much I have accomplished greatness. I may have stored
myself away on a shelf for some time but obviously I needed to. For
whatever reasons I became silent in my past which was needed to
actually strengthen my reasons for listening and making me now
aware. As I slowly grasped the ring of awareness through the years,

I strengthened my own path towards growth. There is an inner light in all of us that at times dims but never ever goes out totally. It is when it is ignited to its brightest that true happiness is possible. As Spiritual Beings we are all bearers of this light. I was a light for Gracie during her darkest times and I was not even aware of it. Still my love warmed her enough to allow her to live a life where she felt loved. Everyone needs to feel loved and accepted. Look at your life and around those who you know – is there anyone you can shine your light on?

My mothering skills have always been my greatest strengths and this is why my children chose me. In thinking in the past that I may have done something wrong, I am learning I did right by my children. Today they thank me for being their mother. They are grateful as they adore me for I adore them as well. I feel this in my inner soul the love they carry for me. I am thankful to God that I always followed my gut reactions when it came to my children for this did me well. Live and let live is another motto I have learned about recently. I am not claiming here that I was a perfect mother because I did have my moments of tears and vulnerability but I have learned that I am the most stable person for my children in their lives. I have never changed that part of myself because I have no doubts as to how I am a mom for them. I am sure if you spoke to each of my children you would get different descriptions of me but all in all they know they are loved unconditionally by me.

Neither I nor anyone is capable of changing another is what I have learned as I travelled this amazing journey. Everyone needs to be themselves. We are all on our own path in life that will eventually bring us to the choices we need to create a life we can live with and love. It is what we choose to learn and accept in life that makes a difference. When you are filled with the knowledge and belief to help others, as well as yourself, you're being given the gift of trust that can allow love in and insight into the world as a whole. With this gift we learn the meaning of true love. Emotions are a part of everyone's life and we push them deeply away from the surface. Are we that afraid to feel alive?

My strength and belief in myself shall create the life I choose to live. As I listen to myself I realize all that has gone, all that is now, and all that is to come. Materially there is not one thing I need or crave for. Peace and happiness is all that is needed to live a joyous, loving existence. With the strength of my desire to be a person that enlightens others I shall succeed in becoming a known author. The word of God mixed with love is a recipe that is to be shared by me. I feel it. I know it. I shall accomplish it.

With the strength I now possess I have grown and changed to be a blossoming flower as I have been told. I was closed and hanging low but now I turn to the sun and open up my petals to drink in the warmth I have needed. As I create, my light will glow brightly for happiness will fill my being. I will accomplish spreading and comforting those who are lost and fearful themselves. I know this feeling. I had unhappiness and despair every day for I filled with fear in my life yesterday. I know how silence hurts and mental abuse carves one up. At one time I had been able to feel bitterness, hatred, anger, loneliness, emptiness, despair, and a constant fear. I put a mask on to show the world that all was well. I survived by beating myself up and believing that I was of no importance. In a way in not asking anything of others just by trying to please others I survived and did not need to understand or comprehend the life I lived. Acceptance is a lesson I learned early in life by Gracie.

The struggles I fought daily within myself were no different than Gracie's which I am able to realize today. Loving parents are needed by all of us. A crazy mom or a mom who does not want to love her child is scary for any age child. The need for love, peace, and a calm, safe family unit I craved as much as Gracie did. Children do learn from what they are taught and what they see. The strong child is the one that no matter what follows their own heart in life. We can find that child within at any age and search for what our heart needs to survive. Look within and begin your search and find your insight. Releasing the past because it cannot be changed is true forgiveness. Move on and find that which creates your freedom from yesterday as I have done.

The negativity of yesterday that I believed erased God from my life as I filled with these ugly emotions is the air of insight today. Now that I have found love these ugly emotions are no longer part of my life. The emotions of today are happiness, joy, and excitement. To be fulfilled is to accept you are not alone.

Once I started to devour knowledge and reading all that I could get my hands on that dealt with diet, massage, reiki, meditation, prayer, and my own health, I became deeper and deeper involved in a holistic lifestyle. I see how special life can be when we are able to change and see the past as steps to the future. To get here today, I had to crawl, walk, and run through yesterday. To approve and love myself now I had to struggle through the dark time of pain first. I feel almost dazed with this knowledge. To stay focused as I learn and listen to be aware of every thought, word, and action in a positive manner brings me closer to my destiny.

Insight has been shown to me as I began to soul search and became witness that the little girl from yesterday had grown to be a woman waiting for her time. I am proud of her for holding on. At times I was deeply saddened at the struggles she had to face back then. The tears I have shed through the years can most likely fill an ocean. The only constant in my life as a child and as a grown woman had been Gracie. She never faulted or strayed from who she was. Her wisdom was her strength and how wonderful that I was able to choose her, this amazingly wise woman, as my mother. The only regret is that I did not know Gracie as a child; if I had, I would have loved her then too.

Chapter Seventeen

Love

I am filled with warmness
As I experience a closeness
Can this be the gift of truth?
For I can no longer be mute
Wonderment has made me stronger
Knowledge is filling my hunger
To nourish my soul must begin
As I gather my thoughts from within
Yesterday's pain has disappeared
I am filled with the gift of love to hear
Thank you, God, for erasing the fear

Today I can exist in life with loving all who cross my path on a daily basis. Yet, yesterday I was capable in life of not loving myself. We are all guilty of letting chores and responsibilities take over. As we forget this tiny little ingredient in life called love, we silently starve ourselves. Once we accept the nourishment necessary to feed a starving soul is love, we change from within. Somehow we forget to take care of ourselves insisting that we are not important. We allow ugly words to strike us down. We watch life pass us by believing we are of no value or that we have no rights. I question if this is a mothering thing handed down to daughters or just the society we grow up in.

Generations of women before today have fought for the right of equality and still in this time and age there are those of us who cringe at the slightest thought of independence. It's scary beyond belief that there are still women in this day and age that are victims of their fathers, husbands, boyfriends, and men they work with who believe women are less important than men.

I survived childhood living in a home that I was not aware of being dysfunctional. A father that believed he was simply better than my mother or any woman. His negativity and words of disbelief that she could possibly know anything enabled him to shatter her life. Love for my mother Gracie was simply honesty, acceptance, obedience, and dedication. She lived with the idea of devotion as her main ingredient. For her, love equaled devotion; this is what she based her own beliefs on. She grew up in a time and place where the wife waited at home sparkling and clean with dinner on the table as she hushed the children so as not to upset their father upon his return from a day at work. After all, the home was his castle and as the king he required respect and worship.

The mind is more powerful than any of us gives it credit for. The thoughts we think daily are constant. We are able to drive ourselves mad by this mere fact in life as I have written. Why does a mother choose to neglect her child and dedicate herself to a man instead? What is the reason we exchange our power and belief of our own dreams so that a man can be happy as we hand over ourselves when we marry and why? The act of a strong man truly loving and accepting a woman on her own path in life is far and few in past generations. Have we accomplished for the women of today to learn from the women of yesterday? I don't believe so because we do not communicate and support one another. I do not believe any longer that anyone is stronger than another. I believe that anyone is capable of loving more in any relationship. As we learn in life we grow and stumble without realizing that the choices we make are creating our own path and existence that will fulfill us individually.

The old saying that "no one knows what goes on behind closed doors" is true for all. Most women today turn their backs on one another because we are raised to believe we are required to answer only to our husbands. We become ashamed without realizing it and hide behind the faces we show to one another. We play a part and wear a mask for the world to see. Those who crumble at the hand of a man cannot understand the abuse inflicted on them. They believe they have done something wrong and deserve to be mistreated by their loving husband or man in their lives. There is verbal abuse as well as physical and emotional abuse that scars us and breaks us into little pieces as we crumble within. We must remember we are all created equal and no one has the right to inflict pain on another.

There is a world of knowledge waiting for all of us. We try to do the best we can and are thankful every day we survive. Life is not meant to be this hard. There is no reason to live in a world filled with pain and fear from yesterday, today, or tomorrow. I myself lived a life that was tumultuous. I loved my mother deeply and in the end was rewarded by sharing my love with her. Gracie to me had always been a lost soul. The other life I showed to the world I chose to camouflage. I accepted my life because I believed in love like Gracie. Gracie felt that if she loved it was right so I too chose to believe that I loved deeply enough to make it right.

After her death I have written how I felt confused and lost myself. I loved my husband and my children but I felt that I was missing something with Gracie no longer being part of my life. I hadn't realized how attached I had been to her and our visits through the years. There had to be a better way to live life for me to achieve, for I doubted I could go on much longer. I dappled with the thoughts of suicide like Gracie at one time – to just end my life and the pain I lived through daily by the abusive language I was witness to. I did not want to feel the pain of death or the realization that I accepted abuse in the manner of daily verbalization from people who said they loved me. I began to question if I accepted this because I grew up with my father verbally abusing my own mother. In reading Gracie's words, I saw myself. I began a search to heal. I needed to know of the reason I existed. Gracie believed my reason had been to teach her that unconditional love was possible in her lifetime.

I asked myself where I would begin such a search. A lover of the written word, I chose to read books about the different religions of the world. I went back to the roots of my own life and started with reading the Bible and any book I could find on the Blessed Mother. I was intrigued by Zen, Buddhism, and Kabbalah. I enjoyed the words I read and began to think differently about life. In the end I chose to turn my devotion and prayer towards the Blessed Mother. As I prayed for support and spoke to her I asked her for guidance in my life and begged her to be my mother now that Gracie was gone. I felt lost, alone, and tremendously fearful. Tears would wet my pillow as I begged for help and love from someone. I wanted so much to feel loved during this time and I could not find anyone to accomplish this feeling for me. I connected at once with her strength and the love the Blessed Mother offered to me. I prayed to be a good wife and mother to my children and to understand my husband's fears. I knew she would look over my children from the heavens for I was not always with them and worried less now that I prayed to her. I began to feel less alone in life and wrote the following words in gratitude:

"O Holy Mother, I feel your breath surrounding me as I tremble in the night. Praying for your strength and guidance to enlighten me! My fingers travel gently along the rosary beads as I pray the words to bring you near, for you comfort me. At times I am troubled and scared. I turn to you as I shed a tear. When I am filled with darkness you are my bright light. The beauty of your image is like no other. There is only one Blessed Mother."

I found today that my path finally has returned to me the gift of love, belief, and prayer. Raised a Catholic as a child I drifted away from the routine of a life shared with God. I became too busy for Him. Now that I searched and found I was not alone I am able to appreciate God as part of my life because I know He is in my life. Once I heard God's whisper of love for me and chose to love myself, my life path became my journey. I awaken with thoughts and words to God; I spend my day with thoughts and words to God, and I end my day with thoughts and words to God.

With this foundation of love as the power to set me on my journey, I chose to nourish my soul. Books called out to me to be read. I listened to the desires that made sense to me. I craved this ability to find answers and knowledge. I began my journey and constantly asked myself, what am I to be? I was reading so many books on life that I felt I was being told something. I had a destiny to fulfill. There was a time that I had such pain inside that I feared I had not left anything behind to help another. I did not know how to help another. It was time for me to find out if I had a passion inside that would rise that I could accomplish. Fear was my constant at that time and something I had no idea on how to erase.

Like everything I have always done in my life I simply moved forward reading books that appealed to me. I read so many books on diet that I wondered if I was to be a nutritionist but I could not see myself as such. I became consumed by a Spiritual/Holistic lifestyle as I traveled into books on soul work and meditation. At my fingertips I surrounded myself with books upon books to read. I desired an alternative way of life to live, compared to the life I had always lived prior to today. Excitement like a child waiting for her birthday greeted me every waking moment. Through backtracking my own personal writing I learned an undercurrent of Spirituality had always been part of my existence waiting for me to embrace it.

Why we become so busy in our lives that tomorrow must wait for us to fulfill our own dreams is a mystery to me. How many of us never take the time to seek that which would truly make us happy? All anyone needs to do is to find love within and your life path reveals itself. Everything in life will fall into place. The past, present, and the future have been set. Love is capable of revealing the little moments in life that are offered that we refuse to take. I believe that in the past I became so wrapped up in the despair of my life that I clung to it as a safety blanket because I did not know how I would feel without it. I defined myself by this despair created by mental abuse towards me. I could not understand why I was treated in such a manner but I was curious enough to stay and learn from it.

We have become a society that has time to make money, buy houses and cars, children to raise, chores to perform, but no time to accomplish our own dreams. You simply learn to let life rule the way. To remember your dreams and strive for them is to find love for yourself. With love as the foundation to be, everything else on our path will brighten and glow as it lightens the way. When I discovered that I LOVED MYSELF, literally the doors of heaven opened. Learning what is important allowed me to experience the greatest of feelings for myself.

Love is the major key. To fill with love for yourself enables you to be true to your self first. With this belief that it is fine to laugh, share, and comfort others, we are then filled with love totally. This enables only truth into our lives. The hardest part is to be true to what is important in life. Life is filled with assumptions and strife. Daily we want to be heard. Why is it so hard for one to listen and learn? A question we need to ask.

These changes I have slowly accepted as part of who I am to be is all about what Gracie was missing in her life and what I was missing in my life as her daughter. The power of love is strong beyond what one can ever imagine. I have been guided to fill these pages with a daily reminder that the most important thing anyone can do for themselves is to find the love within that is waiting to be embraced. To be honest and truthful is as important and necessary in one's life as is love.

When you are filled with love, a single lie can produce a beam of darkness. Once we correct a lie and fill with the bright light of love again we are nourishing our soul. The whole package is love, honesty, truth, peace, health, and happiness as a bright light that fills us. When we lie, hate, fight, steal, are mean, or angry, we fill with darkness. We can never be a bright light and darkness at the same exact moment. When we choose to fill with the brightness of light we choose a soulful path as our existence. We choose simply to love. We become one with the universe and we trust the process of life because we believe. The whisper of our soul fills us with calmness which leads us to be honorable.

Finally, my soul cried out to me so loudly that I listened. As my thoughts changed and I read all I could a change for me began to surface. As I actually paid attention to myself, I chose to walk along this new path with a passion. I was very interested in finding a better way of living and existing finally in a meaningful life. Slowly I erased my fear without realizing that it was no longer. I was filling with love. The awareness of being in the presence of love and realizing I am not alone has fulfilled me totally which enables me to continue on. I am evolving so fast that I am able to appreciate different aspects in my life better. I wasn't aware of how happy I really have been. My struggle seems to be dealing with negativity from others which today I am learning to accept.

I ask myself this question: "How could one ever be depressed, hateful, or angry about anything if they let love in?" Love is everywhere we look – the plants, the trees, the sky, the land, the water, the rain, the sun, the snow. The wonder of nature in reality is simply Mother Nature taking care of us and comforting our days with her beauty if we choose to pay attention. All of this plus the animals, birds in the trees, and the people we meet on the street are love. We are all surrounded with this gift of beauty daily. It could be a little tree in bloom or covered in snow, maybe the beauty of snow crystals on all the tree branches, or raindrops dripping down the windshield. If we took the second it takes to appreciate the wonder of it all, we would be joyous. Become aware of those around you and the benefits of beauty will be seen. A woman's lips as she smiles at her baby or speaks gently of the love for her parents or a twinkle in someone's eye as they share a loving caress with another – all are miracles of life. Even a baby's cry for help is filled with trust and love that someone will come and hold him.

Everyone's tree of life has many branches that can be watered daily. The branches on my tree of life I have named Love, Respect, Compassion, Kindness, Joy, Gratitude, Reiki, Massage, Meditation, Prayer, Organic Foods, and Positive Thoughts. When I believe my tree is in bloom I will know because I will be sharing and helping others. My tree of life will be full by this final accomplishment.

Once everyone loves inwardly themselves and outwardly the world, they become centered in their beliefs. I am not talking about Christianity, Religion, or Church but the total complete feeling of love throughout one's body. This change makes all the difference in your mind and thought process. You cannot be hateful, mean, and deceitful when filled with love. To change towards love is the greatest experience that is given to us. We are all born with this feeling as babies, and when we are on our true path it is returned for us to experience. In accepting God as the One and Only we then accept love into our lives. I pray that all at sometime feel the power of the strength of this love.

On the path of change you become aware of all living creatures that you must believe are needed to learn the lesson of compassion from. Humility comes to us when we let in the feeling of sight and belief that even an "ant" has a right to his life. Respect for ourselves encourages you to respect all you have and all that others are capable of having. Creativity is a gift to us which is ours when we smile in the morning and look forward to the day for we love our existence and all that we choose to accomplish. This is because we are walking the path towards fulfillment and making the dreams of yesterday true. Those of us who believe know in our hearts that all we have is a gift that enables our belief and ability to stay focused on our path. We fall victim to the belief we are alone and must do it all. In reality all we need to do is believe enough to call out for help. Once we believe in ourselves and all that we are, everything else our heart desires will be able to come true. Trust the Divine Intelligence that has created who we are, and all that we can accomplish will be provided.

God has installed in us a compass that we need to use with our map to return to Him fulfilled. This compass is different in the aspect that it does not have South/North or East/West. Our interior compass has Love/Belief and Hate/Fear. When we follow the arrow towards love and belief we will find our path. Those of us who choose fear and hate will not return home to God's love yet. They will return to a life here on earth until they learn. This is the belief of reincarnation. One must strive to get it right to find their true path. God has great patience and will wait forever if it takes that for us to learn our lessons. I have learned that balance is needed in life and that in the end we choose even to be re-born to help another to create a shift from fear to love in their next lifetime. I believe that there are no mistakes and that the bottom line is to be born to live a loving, good, and happy life helping one another, no matter what.

God does work in mysterious ways and it is not Him but our own choices that create what we must learn. Many believe that God gives us only that which we can handle. What God gives us is free will, period. To learn the lesson of Tolerance is to be and accept our path, no questions asked. We become tolerant of peace or no praise; of love or no love. Once we learn tolerance we accept the life we are given and run with it. We believe it is a good life, no matter what struggles we live through. It is not a life for us to question; it is a life we choose to live and learn from. Once we can absorb that we are here for a lesson to be learned we shall find happiness. It is amazing that the entire process we call life is a lesson. To believe in ourselves, to trust our instincts, to know of the choices we can make are all within. We bury these feelings because we look for an easy way out. There is none. Life is about lessons that we need to learn to grow and expand our soul.

When we are born we have no knowledge of money, only love; then temptation in the form of monetary value takes over eventually as we grow up. We move in a different aspect of our lesson – one which will find a way to return ourselves to our original choices. All in all we are learning through life all of the time.

There are so many different lessons to learn: Truth, Honesty, Tolerance, Patience, Peace, Love, Respect, Acceptance, etc. What have you learned so far? Think of the moments you filled with despair, pain, humiliation, guilt, and regret. These emotions are simply lessons in life that one needs to learn to continue towards their destiny.

Joy is an emotion that lets us find happiness with ourselves. Therefore we are happy for others too. How could we not be when we experience the feeling of love entirely through us not for a little bit or just for a day but for eternity? Eternity is very important for that is when we will finally be home, having consumed our true lives.

Our souls are eternal. We do not see them here on earth. The body is a vehicle we drive while on this planet. It will be junked and discarded when we are to return home. If we have nourished and filled our souls to the brim with love, then our soul returns home in the true light of love. Our soul does not die. Even if we commit suicide our soul quickly finds another vehicle to incorporate itself into and once again whatever pain we carried before returns until our lesson here on life's planet Earth is learned. I have learned that karma is actually the memory from a previous lifetime that we had not learned from. Maybe we just ran away from the lesson, divorced the husband, and abandoned the child. Whatever the pain during this lifetime we can make peace now by finally allowing love in.

For whatever reason anyone finds it necessary to end their own life, all that you succeed in doing is killing your body (the vehicle) and not your soul. Immediately upon the junking of the vehicle (the body) you are reborn on earth into another one with the same soul. You will then return to live the exact same life until you learn your lesson which is, simply, love. There is a theory that all death is a suicide after all because no one dies unless they are ready to die and move on, whether that is through illness or by their own hands. The power of thought creates the illness which is then aggravated by the foods and drink consumed and whether or not one's DNA has also been part of their process and belief.

We all need to remember that with love there is no fear – only love. The angry, hateful, miserable, abusive person is full of fear. Fear of the unknown, fear of needing more, fear of the need for power; money is very important to these people, and these desires are needed to keep the vehicle functioning. This inner fear creates a vehicle that is dirty; you need to change the oil, wash and clean the outside, and put the best fuel in to help it run properly along the path in life by following your own compass.

Once you accomplish nourishment for yourself, you admit love for yourself and you then see life through the eyes that are now filled with love. Everyone and anyone who chooses to change can. Dig deep inside for the spot where you can be the happiest. This spot fills you with the gift of creativity to be who you are meant to be.

When we are witness to ourselves being capable of achieving all we can be, we find love. God is love. Unfortunately, we are consumed with love for the wrong things in life. This love builds up so fast that it takes over and erases what we need to do. This need to keep our dreams alive can only be accomplished by us being true to ourselves.

If you are creative and filled with love and joy in your life, everything that is possible will come to you. To trust life is a lesson to be learned. God's plan is never revealed to us unless we cry out to Him for His guidance, support, encouragement, and strength. We must without questions trust the life we are living because the end result is eternity when we find and accept love.

Love and hate are opposites. To love is not, as they say, "this day thing" or "maybe next month" type of feeling. To love is complete, total, all-day belief and relief that all is possible. You cannot find love if you are filled with hate. God is waiting to see our reactions, choices, and needs. Life is filled with tests that get us through the journey so that we believe in the end in God. Society and generally the life we live put it to sleep. We are the only ones who can awaken ourselves. We can choose to awaken at any time, at any age, by searching for a better life.

You do not wake up and suddenly are different. Change is gradual for all. It is the little realities of life that change us. This can be a simple test of true forgiveness and forget. For this is love. Another test is to accept we are responsible for our vehicle – no one else. I myself changed tremendously when I released the need to put poison, toxic foods, inside of me. By choice I stopped eating meat. In doing so, I awakened a connection so profoundly sensible that I filled with laughter daily. I opened the air waves to let God in. I am no longer clogged, bloated, confused, or depressed because the toxins have been erased from my body. My vehicle is shiny, clean, and has premium fuel to keep it running smoothly. Pay attention to your body and it will reveal what it needs.

Today as I think back to the toxins that filled Gracie I cringe. The medications alone had to harm her body and create an empty feeling inside. The foods she consumed were not of the best quality and what she could consume had to be very soft because she had no teeth to chew. Ice cream, puddings, chocolate, and applesauce were her staple foods. It makes me wonder if the foods and chemicals we ingest have something to do also with mental illness. That is why I know for sure that Gracie needed the lesson of love to complete her because not only was she filled with toxins and a poor diet but she smoked as well. Yet, she always stood true to her beliefs that love is the glue needed to survive.

To truly love is an everyday experience. Love is needed to be like the air we breathe to live. Love is to be the nourishment one needs to survive. Love is to be the water we cleanse ourselves with to shine. Love is to be the moment we are awake, while we sleep, and the moment we start our day. When we choose to love life and those who are part of our lives we are at peace. Love is an expression that we throw out to one another without really feeling its warmth. Love and being are the little things in life we do for each other.

We love our parents but we're too busy doing what we want to do to take a second to do something for them. We love our children but we are too busy to sit and listen to them or to just spend time together. Husbands and wives love one another but are so engulfed in the power game that they tend to try and control one another and change each other. Love is found in the little cherished moments of life – sitting, reading, talking about whatever matters to that child we love. Spending time to put a smile on an elder parent's face that will take us away from doing something we want to do just because we love and appreciate all they have done for us. Husbands and wives that truly love and accept each other as they are (fat, tall, skinny, short); their lives and what they can be for one another is more important than anything else. Kissing, hugging, talking, laughing, and remembering are all expressions of love. They all cost us nothing but time. This is a lesson we all need to learn. When we can give of ourselves truly and honestly for another with no questions asked, just because we love them and want to be part of their lives. The gift of time is true happiness for us as well as those we give it to. God has no use for a monetary gift from us. The gift that counts to God is the one that shows Him love.

To love yourself and to love your neighbor by helping them is tremendously approved of. To sit and visit an elder parent is an expression of love. To talk and listen to a troubled teen without judging them is love. To visit someone who lives alone and try to comfort them is love. To care for another besides you is love. To love openly all without criticism or judgment is love. To volunteer and be of service to anyone is an act of love. That is what is important to live a fulfilling, healthy, productive life. God is waiting for all of us as a society to find the love within and focus on it. Life is not about who we are or what we believe is important. Life is about loving, sharing, doing, and helping others. Inside of all of us there is love. It is just stuffed so far down that we cannot feel it. We as a society put a price on everything. The more expensive a gift means it is a better gift. When the one gift that is the best gift to give and to receive is free and its name is love.

In reality the message is that one cannot just read the books, meditate, pray, or do yoga and then expect a new way of life. To awaken one day changed and to feel free like a bird is to participate in the life we are given. To live for today, forgive tomorrow and any mistakes we feel we have made or others have created in hurting us. Open your heart to all that can be. Your every thought, action, word, and feeling daily, weekly, monthly, and yearly to the point of being intuitive and letting God guide you forward is the only way to live. We are all capable human beings because in essence we are Spiritual Beings that need to dig deep within and detoxify our bodies, minds, and souls and find our own clarity.

Try to remember the Gracie of yesterday and how she cracked under the pressure of no love. Her mom left her; her husband left her, and she went insane under the pressure of no love. Through the years she learned and accepted with open arms the love I was able to share with her. In the end she died, alone and with no material possessions of her own; she did die happy because she knew how it felt to feel loved because in me she saw a light that led her out of her darkness.

Chapter Eighteen

Nourishment

I need to do this for myself
I need to find solace
I need to feel silence
Within me runs a current of energy
That desires to be ignited
As I create the flame shall light itself
And burn brighter for all eternity
God will accomplish this dream to nourish me
As I spread His love through my creativity

Aromatherapy – Bath – Candle – Dance – Exercise
– Incense – Journaling – Massage – Meditation –
Music – Prayer – Reiki – Sing – Walk – Yoga!

These are all considered nourishment for us. Diffusing oil or lighting incense or a candle changes the energy around you and places a smile on your lips. Close your eyes and breathe in the smells of the oil or the scent from the candle and let the silence bring you relaxation. Take a moment to visit your Church or Temple during the day and feel the stillness and quiet, cool essence that lingers in the air. A five-minute quick hello to God and you become filled with a sweet calmness. Even better, soak in a bath that at the same time has a few drops of oil and release the day to the universe. Take a walk on the beach as the sun warms your face; hear the birds sing as the spray of water from crashing waves delights your senses with the smells of fresh air, salt on your lips, and the feeling of fulfillment enters your soul. By taking paper and pen, be witness to your accomplishments and dreams as your inner consciousness is revealed to you and the warmth of your own words brings you the power to be. Sit silently breathing in and out with your eyes closed emptying yourself of thoughts and emotions to be enlightened and encouraged forward. Play soft music in the background as you do your chores, calming your senses while incense fills your senses with awareness. Light candles at dinner or in your bedroom as you sit and relax reading this book or for that matter any book that is spiritual for 15 minutes a day. Dance to lift your spirits and sing to put laughter into your soul. This is what I can call nourishing myself by being aware of that which strengthens my purpose while allowing me to fill with more love for me than food can ever accomplish.

As they say, we need water to live but food is not as important. A fruit, piece of bread, some brown rice, maybe a sweet potato, salad with vegetables, free-range meat, or wild fish; then throw in beans and nuts for dessert; these will suffice it as the nourishment a body needs. This was the basic diet that generations before us all survived on in life. Many of us are consumed by the foods that we eat and allow these choices to rule us from the moment we awaken every day. The first question of the day is: "What are we going to eat for breakfast, lunch, and dinner today?" Food is a constant thought for many.

Somewhere along the path of life, knowledge, and invention, plus the power of money, we replaced the reality of necessity. Fast food and the world of processed foods have created a new need we desire and belief that these foods nourish our bodies. Our tastes have replaced our requirements. From the world of candy, cookies, ice cream, cakes, and potato chips, we have filled buildings that we call today supermarkets with an enormous amount of unnecessary cravings and desires. The taste of sweets has overruled an entire nation of people. There was a time when one chose a piece of fruit to quench the need for something sweet. Today we no longer think of what we put into our mouths. There is such a variety to choose from; we choose that which is not true nourishment but that which tastes good. We have become a nation crippled by the belief that if it is in a store it is to be eaten.

To get back to basics one must think and believe the following: "If it grows from the ground or from a tree, then I can eat it." We decided through the process of growth to eat out of cans and bags and that fast is a better way. We live in the world of processed foods that are empty of nourishment for the body. One day we awaken and no longer recognize the person we have grown enormously to be. We search the aisles of bookstores for a new way, a new book, a new diet, a pill, or anything that can get us back to what we were at another time. Temporarily, we are tricked into a protein diet, a low-carbohydrate diet, fat-free diet, fasting, or simply denying that which our body truly needs. Life is full of the need to change and grow for all of us. We believe what is written in diet after diet to erase the fears we cannot stop because we doubt ourselves.

I myself was one who tried every diet that was offered to the American public yesterday. I wanted a quick fix to the body I hated. I never realized the true value of nutrition. I stumbled onto the path of holistic nutrition and the belief that juicing and eating living foods mostly was the way to go for me. Finally, something in my brain clicked – "wow," I look and feel this way by the toxins I am eating, the processed foods, and the animals that are injected with hormones and chemicals today. I tried juicing first and have to admit it was hard. I needed to chew, but I felt clean. Then I tried a raw-food diet and found that I needed to eat cooked foods but I was able to eliminate all meats. I missed my broccoli. Today I am proud to say I enjoy how I look and feel healthy by the choices I eat daily. I juice and eat fruits, vegetables, potatoes, rice, grains, and nuts daily, as well as cold-water fish a few times a week. I actually enjoy a cup or two of coffee in the morning as well. Recently I literally fell in love with yogurt and enjoy yogurt in the morning in the colder months with walnuts as my breakfast. I love a really good salad, and I love pasta. I eat foods that make me feel good and that I enjoy. I bless every morsel that goes into my mouth and thank God for nourishing my body with these foods I am eating. I am a true believer that if you eat foods that you love and enjoy you will eliminate guilt and just eat to live, period. So much energy is placed on the foods by the categories we have placed on them which mostly stem from two words: this is bad or good for me. There is an inner thought that is creating the weight more than the food that is eaten. Find that out and release the need to eat foods that put on weight because you actually believe that they are.

The biggest change I made in my life which cut down on an enormous amount of unhealthy foods was the elimination of trans fats from my diet. I became an avid reader of labels. I refused to eat anything that had this one ingredient in it. I was amazed to find that it was in every food in the supermarket that we all eat and never realized the damage we are doing to our bodies.

Deanna M. Minich, Ph.D., C.N. has written the book, An A-Z Guide to Food Additives, Never Eat What You Can't Pronounce. Studies indicate that eating these fats (partially hydrogenated oil or trans fats) have serious adverse health outcomes. They increase risk for heart disease by increasing "bad" (LDL) cholesterol and decreasing "good" (HDL) cholesterol. There is no safe amount of trans fat that is allowed. Other health effects relating to cancer, diabetes, infertility, and weight gain remain under investigation. Since 2006, the amount of trans fats in a product can be found in the Nutrition Facts labeled under the fat category. If the ingredient list shows that the product contains "partially hydrogenated oil," chances are it also contains trans fat.

I also eliminated dairy from my diet except for organic low-fat or skim milk that I put in my coffee. I simply cannot drink black coffee. That was the first step in becoming aware of how my body reacted to foods I ingested. After reading an accumulation of books on nutrition and changing how I eat, I lost weight, which was a greatly important aspect in proving that I was eating foods that I chose to believe were bad for me. In continuing my new way of eating now I have sustained my weight to what I am happy with and feel good about, as well as healthy about.

After I left the teen years of my life my body began to change and the lowest I ever weighed had been 115 pounds and for me that was a small size. Then motherhood and dealing with stress and trying to protect myself from abuse I blossomed to 190 pounds at 5'0." I did not like what I saw in the mirror. I did not like how I felt. I cried and hid if a wedding or party came up. I was very conscious of my weight because I was constantly told that I WAS FAT! If I never looked in a mirror I could imagine I was perfect as I was but that is impossible, and when I felt horrible because I had no self-esteem I wallowed in my own self-pity. I wanted to be thin and lose weight but I continued the yo-yo dieting syndrome for years. They say it is hereditary but everyone in my family including Gracie was slim and tall. I saw Gracie's weight plummet up and down because of the medication and the junk she thrived on.

I was hungry for love or maybe just a kind word from those I loved so I stuffed myself with the wrong foods over and over again through the years. Many of us have a hole inside caused by some form of traumatic experience or abuse in our lives. Food is the medication of choice to fill the hole and in the end we cannot release the pain from the fear of never being thin again. Journaling, meditation, and walking, as well as Reiki, are avenues to consider finding the shovel that dug the hole in the first place. I write this today because those are the methods that changed my life so to speak. When I would take a serious look at my life and all that I desired to be as far as my weight, I knew that I wanted to be a healthy and slender grandmother to be able to play with the babies of my future. Today I am nourishing my body, mind, and soul by the choices I choose to eat because I enjoy them and I feel good while eating them.

Shelves and shelves of food are in stores sitting for us to buy them whether they are healthy or not. Why, because we can. Does anyone ever really read the ingredients to the food they are consuming? Does any mother today realize all the fast food, fast lunches, and ingredients she cannot even pronounce are toxic? These toxic ingredients that we consume are adding up inside of us daily. We are ingesting chemicals into our own bodies and we don 't care. We believe in our minds that the stores stock these items and they taste good so they have to be healthy for us. Or maybe we just are not aware and eat the foods we eat because we like them. However, if you have a type of anxiety, dis-ease, weight problem, or sleep problem, start to read labels. I beg each of you that are reading this book, read labels and start by eliminating one ingredient only: trans fats or partially hydrogenated fats/oils in any food that you consume.

All of the illness and diseases of today can be erased if we cared enough about our own bodies and the thoughts we create over and over. If you love yourself, then you also love your body and what you put inside of it. We have ourselves made the rules up that we live by. We have created an acceptance to the belief that a diet – whether it be all protein, all fats, low carbohydrates, or shakes – is acceptable as a form of nourishment. We'll even try a pill thinking maybe that would work because it is fast and easy. What is needed is to learn and educate ourselves about what we are eating. We live by the vicious cycle of wanting the taste of un-nourishing food versus the taste of healthy, nourishing foods.

I found for myself that I refused to be a number for I am more than that and then I decided that I would cleanse my body two times a year by juicing and then I decided no foods were bad but that I would experiment and find the foods that I enjoyed that were healthy for my body and here I am today. We must, I beg of you, change our thoughts about food, as well as our taste buds, for the healthy choices in life and live a highly productive existence well past our nineties and beyond by the choices we make.

Fruit, a natural enjoyable food that can be grown organically, is a healthier choice by far than cookies and processed cakes. Cold-pressed organic extra virgin olive oil is healthier for us than the trans-fat varieties in margarine and butter that are cancerous and not good for us to consume. The meats we are given as a choice to eat are poisonous today to our bodies. They are injected with hormones, pesticides, and whatever makes for a heavier, more productive animal. Take mad-cow disease. We are eating a cow that has died because it was sick and then fed to other animals. Why are we accepting this to be the way for us, the people of a wealthy nation, to be nourished?

A healthy alternative protein-based diet can be obtained from legumes,beans, and nuts. Organically grown broccoli, spinach, carrots, kale – all are healthier. Oatmeal, potatoes, and sweet potatoes are delicious and easier for our bodies to absorb and break down when they are free of chemicals, preservatives, and trans fats. We have become a nation that looks for the fast and easy way out in life. We are killing ourselves and we don't really care to stop or take the responsibility for what we consume.

We have chosen to believe all that we read in the papers and all that we see on television. It is an easier life for us to be accepting if it is advertised to take a pill to lose weight, to lower high blood pressure, to manage one's diabetes; we succumb to this belief. Why are we not told to change whatever we are thinking and eating that is causing this illness and is harming our bodies? The answers are not in a pill because all pills have side effects which do damage to other parts of our body.

To eat healthy is to return to yesterday's eating habits. The days where we had our gardens and bought and consumed only what we needed to eat. We have created a life that puts us as the victims of the processing plants created by us. Look around at your kitchen cupboards. How much waste do you see? How much processed food do you really need? Are there fruits, nuts, and organically grown vegetables visible and part of your diet? The garden of yesterday may be no longer but there are organically grown food sections in the supermarkets to choose from today. Hopefully in time organically grown foods and free-range meats and wild fish will be the only choices to eat. Wash the foods well that are not organic to clean them of the chemicals they are sprayed with.

If all of America would decide today to eat just one healthy meal with no processed ingredients, no chemicals, no toxins and poisons, I promise them they will feel differently and healthier over time. Slowly the need to eat better will be a natural way for all. The days of dieting would end. They would be drawn to a healthier lifestyle only because they would see for themselves the difference in that one meal. Start with one meal and see how you feel; see what happens for the betterment of mankind in choosing different types of healthy foods. Make your water filtered and try not to buy bottled water. Unless you buy water in a glass bottle and recycle by choice, try to remember that plastic bottles have become a huge problem now that the world only drinks bottled water. Believe me, miracles are possible.

When you find true love for yourself, it is a total package you find. Inside and outside becomes beautiful. Try a day at first, once a week, to eat healthy and maybe your thoughts and ideas on life will improve. An apple today may lead to a salad tomorrow, more vegetables, less meat, and less processed foods. Ask yourself one question before you put anything in your mouth: "Is this a processed food?"

We actually need more than food as a form of nourishment. We need to connect with Mother Nature in some way as we live daily. A walk around the block, a stroll at the seashore, fresh flowers brought into the home – all make a difference. Sit and dream of your dreams of contentment in your own backyard surrounded by the life you love. To nourish my body I have learned is to be daring and aware of my own needs. To comfort my soul and nourish its growth I experimented with Reiki. Reiki means universal life force energy. Reiki is just a method of activating and balancing the life force energy present in all living things. Light hand placement techniques are used on the body in order to channel energy to organs and glands to align the chakras (energy centers). It is a technique for emotional and mental distress, chronic and acute physical problems, and for achieving spiritual focus and clarity. This method is used as a means of health maintenance, disease prevention, and healing art and can be applied to oneself and to others. I personally became hooked as I began the process of change slowly. I added massage and meditation to my lifestyle after I learned the comfort of prayer as I have previously written. There was a passion in me to learn everything I could to change totally.

Out of all the changes I made in my life after the death of Gracie, I was to find myself at the water's edge walking in the sand one day. My inner child surfaced jumping up and down and spun me around. I became at that moment so completely nourished in body, mind, and soul that I felt truly blessed. I have been able to open my eyes to the possibility of my own courage and strength, as I have learned the beauty of nourishment is simply listening to the voice within. Going to the beach brings laughter to my heart, love to my face, and peace to my soul at this time. The sky, sea, sand with crashing waves, and birds settle my beliefs. I am where I am meant to be at this time in my life. As I see the sky and look as far as I can out to sea, I appreciate God's ability to fulfill and nourish me if I just pay attention. To be able to appreciate God is to be grateful for all He has given to me.

We as human beings take so much for granted. Everyone must stop, look, and listen to the life they are living. The world is moving very fast with all the technology it can summon. The basics of life have not changed at all though. We may have luxury and money to make us believe these things we need, but nothing can exceed the power your life is able to acquire by the gift of appreciation for Mother Nature. When at the beach, a park, or just sitting in your own backyard, this is where you will be able to find peace. It is not far away or hidden somewhere that we need to search for it. It is within. No electronic device, television, radio, car, or store-bought item, not even food, can give us the gift of peace. With peace, we acquire love of ourselves and others.

The beauty of nature – the sun, rain, snow – are miracles God uses to get our attention. How many times can any of us recall that as we lay out on a blanket in the sand and have exclaimed, "My God, what a beautiful day!" When the rain dampens our world with gray silvery skies where one feels the need to stay at home in the comfort and warmth, we are capable of stating, "I hate this weather." When our mornings are white as we awaken with the beauty of the first snowfall and the glow of a winter storm promises to come, we moan and groan, "It's too cold out." All of these gifts are sent to us from God to remember Him. Look at them as wonders, as the sun warms your face, the rain waters your gardens, and the snow enlivens your day with its beauty. Nourishment is everywhere!

To nourish our souls is free. It costs us nothing. You could try any of the following and learn for yourself:

Prayer

Words of love and honesty spoken and shared with a Divine Being.

"TO PRAY IS TO FEEL LOVED."

Meditation

Silence your mind so you can hear guidance.

"CLOSING YOUR EYES CAN HELP YOU TO SEE."

Respect

Use simple words – I love you, thank you, and please
– to all, which can reflect back to you tenfold.

"TREAT OTHERS AS YOU WISH TO BE TREATED."

Approval

Positivism and love comfort your soul. Practice positive thoughts.

"TO LOVE YOURSELF IS TO LOVE ALL."

Creativity

Everyone has a gift from God within.

"TO BE HAPPY YOU MUST FULFILL YOUR DREAMS."

Faith

Criticism, negativity, and lies drain your energy.

"LIVE AND LET LIVE."

Love

No matter the pain inflicted on you, notice the
pain and fear in your attacker's eyes.

"GIVE ONLY LOVE OR SILENCE, NOT ANGER, IN RETURN."

Laughter

Find joy in your surroundings to smile about as you
laugh out loud at your own accomplishments.

"JOY AND LOVE BRING LAUGHTER TO YOUR SOUL."

Walk

Stroll along and smell the grass, feel the warmth of the sun, go to
the park, the beach, or simply go around the block and be aware.

"BE WITNESS TO THE BEAUTY OF NATURE."

Kindness

Hurt no one: man, woman, child, animal, or plant, physically or mentally.

"TO INFLICT PAIN ON ANOTHER INFLICTS PAIN ON YOU."

To believe that you can do anything with God's love guiding you
could encourage you to trust. God would never allow anything to
stop you from being creative. God supplies the need for creativity
to fulfill our dreams. If you refuse to be creative, then you refuse
happiness and joy in your life. Once you learn to trust, be creative
and believe in yourself – that is when you will move forward. Learn
to say that you do not know the answer to everything. Only God
knows all. To be able to admit is a relief. As a believer in love you
join a world that includes everyone.

Those of us that feel that we are not part of the world but more
like an outsider looking in, as we let life take over and we change

to become what we believe others expect us to be, need to look within. Search for a dream from yesterday and fulfill it. We have no support, no encouragement, and no say in our own lives. We let ourselves believe that we are not special. Why do we choose that we have no right to be ourselves? We erase our identity to become what is expected. Learn to be true to yourself and fulfill your dreams.

Young men of today need to have bodies that are pumped up, and the girls need to be as slim as they can. It is about what one portrays for others to see. Along the way we forget our dreams to be someone that matters to us: a person that we would respect and admire. Instead we choose to live and crave what the beautiful people have, for they have shown us we need to make as much money as fast as we can. The world has fallen corrupt because of these values that are in reality empty and unfulfilling. We place a price on our own lives to gather happiness and love, when all the love we need is within.

To love one another as we would love ourselves. To honor our father and mother! To not steal and commit adultery. Have all these been forgotten? It is a world of material objects and shock values that matter today. The super stars rule the planet while the little girl who feels ugly fills herself up on donuts and candy. Then and only then can she believe she will feel happy. We are a people that move so fast that we need to drive through a restaurant today to eat.

Chapter Nineteen

Balance

As one looks to the blue of the sky
See beyond all that can be
While the blue of the sea fills one
To search within its depths
The vastness of both is the balance of life
That encourages one to be

I need to create a balance in my life today. I am struggling with the peace and quiet as I escape into my own thoughts. I strive to exist in a world of solitude. I notice I am capable of finding happiness by being alone with myself. I am drawn by a force that is greater than me to dream and write that which is being shown to me.

The balance can only be in knowing I am still me. I have not changed and I just have belief now that today I now hunger to find satisfaction by my creativity. The acceptance that I must live as a whole and complete person is a lesson to learn. I may desire the duties of my life as they have always been as I am pulled to a life that is fulfilling. It is the incorporation of all I have learned that is struggling with what was. My eyes are clear to focus on what I need to exist, and to share is now a must. As I find myself at times annoyed with those who are near for it's easy to drift inside of myself to hear. The balance is not a split but more of a joining of my soul and ego. This is the existence of a spiritually enlightened being of quality. As I walk the life path of which I am, doors will open beyond my dreams. The goodness of who I am is the strength today to be able to understand. I need not doubt myself for I am guided by life to walk forward with an inner love that I need to believe is a given by the simple touch of my own hand. To create is the air I need to breathe. To be here now is the beauty of change that fulfills me. I lack or need no material belongings, only this belief to nourish within a balance that can carry me into a life that I was meant to find. Finally I can comfort myself with all that is because I am aware of the clarity of my own existence and need to accept myself as I am in truth in my own heart.

I travel at night to places filled with memories at times and new faces that have no names. Do I search for meaning or awaken and comfort myself with who I am? Hard to recall and even more difficult to make any sense of these dreams, I find comfort in them. Once again a beautiful day awaits me to learn from. My knowledge, insight, and wisdom are all within for me to dig out. Ideas and words struggle to be placed on paper. I look at the pages of a book called Making Believers which needs to be fine-tuned and rewritten in a few spots before I can submit it for publication. I am anxious to get a reaction as I think of who will benefit and enjoy my simple words. To believe or not to believe is my audience. Choosing that a change is needed in one's life is my audience. Geared more for the women of today who feel they are less than the men in their lives is my audience. Those who seek to find love is my audience. I think of the faces and lost eyes of the mentally ill and wonder if the spouses or children filled with pain are my audience.

As I reread my words and remember Gracie I miss her even more. The loss I feel creates a lump in my throat for what had been between us. Being that I wrote this book in two parts it is in essence one lifetime shared by two before they were able to find love. Once the veil of fear gets removed and love is accomplished, you are carried to a life that is strong for with love comes strength. Gracie gave birth to me and in return I gave birth to her in this story that needed to be told for all to seek love in their lives. I, myself, find a rebirthing of who I am to be the rest of my life within this book.

It is up to the choices one makes daily who he or she is. This is the comforting part of the book, for so many of us are not aware that we have a choice. What is expected from us? Only love, joy, happiness, and peace for all. Kindness is a benefit that is extra after we believe we can find love within. To learn that the search is not far but waiting within is the miracle of existence. To be able to fulfill our lives with balance is the lesson that completes the change finally. I myself today struggle and favor the world of purity. I find it hard to watch, absorb, and be witness to the criticism in others. I treasure my solace. I want to hug myself closely and keep the feeling of calmness within warming my soul. I crave to be alone. I treasure the minutes I need to create. I ache to realize all will come in good time. I do not today doubt what I know – it is the words of others who need verification. For I have learned, we are a silly people that do not believe in one another. It is amazing to be witness to the fears of all who struggle so hard not to accept. I can accept balance in my life by just existing as myself and incorporating the side of me that is a given to share. My lifetime has geared me toward this realization – how else can I accept the lessons I learned from Gracie?

I think back to the many women who have shared their lives with me. Wonderful women as in aunts, teachers, friends, mother-in-law, sisters-in-law, and even women in line at the supermarket; but one stands out with the strength of many during a time when women were not allowed to have strength. The balance I am witness to that she created in her life was because she believed and was filled with love. She was capable of listening to her heart and was led by it. She was a beautiful human being while on her spiritual journey and I thank her today for coming into my life for I learned from her as well as loving her own daughter as a soul sister of mine. To be able to appreciate a person like Theresa today who would be acknowledged for her greatness by all fills me with love in my soul for her memory. I recently dreamed of her and she was solid and strong while smiling and approving on the life she looks down on from the heavens. I would like to believe that she watches me as I change and is approving of the Amanda of today. She was a woman of Gracie's age but she was a woman before her time. I imagine that by me knowing her at one time I was able to blossom today and change into finding my own strength in life that I lacked because a little bit of her remained behind with me. It is the beauty of this woman that was a mom and grandmother herself and who loved deeply that encourages me. She was not without trauma or pain in life but she always believed in God throughout it all. Although she was not my mother I had great respect for her as a woman of that generation because she stayed true to herself. To me she was a woman who had grace and handed her gracefulness on to her own daughter. It is a magnificent lesson that was handed down from one generation to another generation that is a wonder for me to be witness of.

By being able to erase the lost girl of yesterday I am able to appreciate that I was unable to exist any longer in that role. The time for change for me was gradual but eventually a part of whom I am to be. I seek today balance in my life for I am aware of the pains, fears, and existence of no hope in others. It touches my soul to be witness to this. The lack of balance in anyone's life creates turmoil and pain that becomes visual.

The problem that is beyond sadness in my lifetime has filled my heart with pain for the overweight people in the world today. I think back to the years when Gracie was obese and unable to even look at herself in the mirror. I question today, what happens? Where does a person slip away to? What dark pit do they fall into that they are unable to find hope and a way out of? I know they are not blind to their own reflection in the mirror. Gracie would cry and not understand why she let herself change so drastically that she was filled with disgust for her own image. I believe like Gracie they are hurting so much inside that they need to bury themselves alive. These bodies that grow beyond recognition are terrified of their own beauty within. Can I dare to make a difference, I ask myself. I only know what I have been witness to with Gracie and the problems I faced in keeping my own weight down. She blew up to an enormous woman and then deflated herself to a woman who was beyond recognition to the normal weight that is healthy. The balance in life that we all need is to be accepting of who we are and believe in what we feel in our hearts. Gracie was unable to see her own beauty for she escaped into a world she craved in her mind. How does anyone begin to teach another that one is beautiful, capable, and special? When in reality they cannot reveal their own inner fears to themselves. They bury them so deeply under the choices they make that they are in limbo.

We all enter into this life as little babies. I would like to know what causes one person to need to escape and hide. Where can a person find the truth in their life enough to warrant a need to chip away at this protection shield they created that is hiding the scared person of yesterday? It is not only about lack of control or dieting as I previously have written. This form of protection that is chosen by them will eventually kill them young as they have accepted to living a life in pain. This protection that they enforce fills them with sorrow that needs to be buried deeply. They are not hungry for food but for a way out of this nightmare they are living in.

Gracie chose a totally different escape from life which I have been able today to learn from. For me I would like to express the words to share with those who are in pain. I am filled with an overwhelming amount of compassion for the women and men I encounter daily that I crave to hug and tell them it is a safe world we live in. Do not be afraid – for you are not alone. These troubled people have no balance in their lives and the society we live in hisses at them. When what they need from us all is love, kindness, encouragement, and support.

In my heart there is a belief that the hunger can and must be satisfied by you searching within to the place you have buried the pain. Maybe journaling upon waking, letting words spill from the heart before eating, or if need be afterwards. I know many who are terrified of hearing their own voice within as it would pour onto the page. Please, I beg of you to try to just write for three pages, and do not even read what you have written for about a month. Miracles are possible. There is no need for a diet immediately to heal and nourish you. Let's start first with changing our thoughts about who we are and nourishing our souls. The balance in this life will be the strength in learning the lesson that you must erase the fears you hold tightly to and love who you are. The process of eating will not be a focus point any longer because you will need less to be satisfied. Gradually walking – just walking – can help with the process of healing. Learning and appreciating to be one with nature is a remedy for all that ails anyone.

We all hide behind the masks of life that fit for us for it is safe to do so we believe. I must admit that it took me years to find my freedom but I have succeeded. I truly believe no one knows another. I find the many thoughts you experience daily is our true choice in life. It is all about what you are capable of thinking.

Anyone like Gracie can choose to escape into their minds and many do. Others have the option of choice instead to benefit from the power of their own minds. I may have had a parent that needed to escape into her mind, but I myself chose to free myself as a victim from myself by using the power and passions of my mind. The belief that my mind could allow complete change by freeing me from fear encouraged in me an enormous ability to believe in myself. I found a new life within waiting for me to live. I found the courage to share what knowledge I have learned with all. I have been gifted with insight that allows me to be. To be satisfied in my own body after all these years and accepting of who I am. I cannot believe at times that I refused to change earlier. To free myself from the fears I was handed down and those I gathered on my own is liberating to the point of complete joy.

There are many people portrayed in this story that Gracie encouraged me to write about. I can only say, do not look to dissect the people but look and learn what and who they were. Their beliefs and love for one another taught them many lessons. I am fortunate from the life I have lived to be able to draw from within a book like this. The significance of this story is true unconditional love. Don't ever think otherwise.

I have been playing with the word balance and having difficulty in not being able to achieve complete balance daily, so I thought. I wonder, what do others see when they look at me? Do I look different to them than I did say ten years ago? What is this magnetism that draws another to see, talk, or touch me? What lies ahead for me that I shall no longer live in the past filled with fear and pain? I have now entered into a world of light as I am driven to accomplish all that

I can. With balance I will accomplish that which has always been within me.

I know that my family feels that I am different and that I have changed. I try to explain to them that I am becoming a better me. I am interested in so much that I read constantly but I still enjoy my chores: the wash, cooking, having family dinner, and celebrating birthdays with them. I do want it all and I do understand at this age they are not where I am, for I was not even at this place when I was their age. So I breathe in and enjoy them all as they are. I have learned we are all at different levels of consciousness and this is okay with me.

There was a time after Gracie died that I had neglected myself to the point of despair. I was so scared. I could not see any resemblance of who I was, never mind who I was destined to be. In freeing myself from this despair and digging deeply for the answers I needed, I learned to spread my wings and fly. I have learned that I am the same child that at ten years old looked at the stars in the sky and knew I was not alone. Life has a way of allowing us to drift but then it pulls us back to safety if we care to learn and experience change of any kind.

This balance I seek and crave has always been – it is who I am. I have just tied up all the loose ends and in doing so have transformed myself into a life that is fulfilled. It is all inside of me this wisdom I have been given. No, I am not crazy, but I am aware of the deep person who lives inside of us all. My balance is my journey that will take me further than I can ever imagine. It is to be that my pen writes these words today, tomorrow, and as long as I am alive.

Chapter Twenty

Satisfaction

My life choices are satisfying my existence today. I eat healthier for the first time in my life. To actually finally learn what to eat at this age amazes me. I nourish myself totally. This power of satisfaction that I possess fills me up and I smile at myself constantly. I smile. I smile. I smile. It seems that at times I find myself chuckling, but I do not know to what, except maybe that I am happy. For I see a person in my reflection that is happy and content to be. My thoughts are positive. My dreams are fulfilling. I look forward to my own life and all that it is. The beauty of satisfaction is that I am in possession of my own strengths and I have learned to hear and listen to myself. My inner beauty is evident for all to see because I am strong in my belief today in myself, so I have been told. Somehow, somewhere, along the way I have been empowered.

I have been given a miracle by the power I now possess in believing in myself. By learning to listen and by becoming aware I feel strong and healthy. As I am attentive to my thoughts I am rich with the knowledge to be honest and truthful at all times. It is a wonder for me to write about the possibility that change can be for all. I am blessed with the feeling to finally be fulfilled in the knowledge I now possess to know of my path and the direction I need to take. My journey has brought me to relish in my power of insight for I know my light is burning brightly. I am consumed by God's love, and I am focused to fulfill my path in this life with Him. To feel a nourished body, mind, and soul I find is comforting to experience as this journey unfolds tenderly and gently daily. All of this knowledge wraps me in the arms of respect for all of life.

Within awaits the confirmation that all of this leads me to the satisfaction I feel daily that I am not alone on this journey nor have I ever been. The fear of loneliness and sadness within me has been replaced by the smile on my lips. I cannot ever go back, from now on I move forward towards the completion of my dreams. I am sharing the life I have lived with you because I truly believe we all struggle through life just as I have. Life is about living and sharing while loving and delighting in it all. As husbands and wives we take a marriage vow that today has no meaning or truth any longer, as I have been raised to see and believe.

My gut feeling is that men form a bond and a secret alliance that is never revealed to us. Women on the other hand are not capable of trust and reaching out for help from each other. Shame is a big belief that many women live with. If you are choosing to disagree with me, please just remember the mask you wear in public. I too wore the mask of despair and sadness at times. It is this mask that becomes a wall separating us from helping one another. Single women steal our married husbands but then our married husbands get away with it all because they have the strength of each other to protect and encourage each other. I am not saying that only men do not stay loyal because we do also stray. Man strays simply because he thinks he must to belong. Men are very loyal to each other and even show their sons that they need not respect their wives by their comments and actions. To live a satisfied life we must trust one another and accept one another. If this is not possible then we need to agree to move on and not cause pain willingly to those we say we love.

You cannot choose to sit back and expect to accomplish love and happiness. There is abuse in the world, neglect, and lack of respect for women. This is the bottom line. I am the third in line as I grew to witness the abuse of my mother and obviously my grandmother's own refusal to acknowledge her child. One must wonder, why? The little I have been told about her can be summed up in the manner in which she died: alone and an alcoholic. Gracie chose to slip away and hide in the world of mental illness. I became silent and believed I was beneath all. When I could not survive anymore in that manner, I dug deeply to find a way out.

This newfound love for me erased the fears of yesterday, as I jumped from change to change in my own life. Somehow through my own life and the guidance that Gracie offered to me I stayed in a roundabout way true to myself. My soul struggled with the belief of fear until I knew to love myself for me. A complete understanding of life has brought me to this exact moment. One can call it the change, menopause, or midlife, but I know it is a combination of the little girl I was that took a few years to live a life that needed to be lived. Now that little girl has surfaced and reminded me of the dreams that I dreamed of so long ago.

I have lived in what I refer to today as the lost generation. Times were very different from today and what the children of today see. Yes, we mock and make fun of those who start their sentences with "I remember when." We could on the other hand try to pay attention and learn from what was. As a child myself growing up, I grew up in a home where both my parents worked which was unheard of back then. Saturday was a day to clean the house, go food shopping, and go to a park or beach, or maybe the movies. Sunday was God's day, a day of rest. One went to Church, to the bakery to get hot fresh bread, rolls, and pastries. A family dinner was prepared and relatives came to visit. If one chose to walk the avenue, as we called it, the stores would be closed, dark, and empty. Sunday was the greatest day of the week and one knew it was a Holy Special Day. Society by choice has erased this day as it had been intended to be. The children of today have no such memory of how beautiful one day a week given to not spending money can make them feel. This feeling was sacred for me when I was growing up. The air even smelled differently on Sunday as I think back on the memory.

Why do we feel the need to work and shop on this one day? In reality we worship money today more than we worship God. Take any Sunday or any day you choose to create a time for your family and experience the beauty of nature we all forget but mostly take for granted. Go to a beach, a park, or just sit in your backyard and read a book. Refuse to spend money on Sunday and see how you feel. Return this day back to a peaceful existence and time for life and living, to stop and smell the roses. Whatever it is you need to buy, can it not be bought during the other six days of the week? It is only one day I am talking about that can and will change your outlook on your own life. Just the process of slowing down one day a week can create miracles.

How are we going to find our paths in life if we cannot give up a simple day to rest? When we erased Sunday from our life as God's day of rest (in the Catholic religion), we went a step further and just erased God from our lives. God does not need one day a week to rest; we need one day to remind us that He exists. We choose not to include God in our lives. Ask yourself one question, "If the America we live in returned to closing all of the stores once again on Sunday, what would happen?" Better yet, simply do not go shopping on Sunday ever again. Think of this as a possible old way of life being reincarnated. A simple way that is easy in reuniting families, love, peace, calmness, and God into the lives of all. To return to a life where we see and are witness to the beauty of nature. To cook a healthy meal and spend quality time as a family one day a week, for there are many that do not share a meal at all during the week. Fun is part of God's plan. Make life fun and meaningful.

A simple conversation I had about buying water in a bottle today brought a smile to my lips for the past. It is strange for the child of today to imagine that when I was a child I drank water out of a faucet. Where did the concept come from that water is no longer free and we need to buy it? Not only do we buy it in the stores everywhere, but also we can have home delivery of it. The truth needs to be known that these little bottles filled with water that we drink are harming our planet – please recycle them or just get a water filter!

We are all unique individuals capable of so much. Along our path towards our destiny we have all become overshadowed by money. How much money can we make? How much money can we spend? Can we not accomplish this in six days, especially with computers now? We don't even need to leave our houses to go shopping.

If only one person in a hundred that is reading this would STOP. Be the individual that God created and choose to hear His voice today. Imagine what you will hear and be able to accomplish. We have become a people who have willingly erased our own unique individuality. We are consumed by material objects and what we can buy with money. How much money do we need to be happy? In reality money cannot and never will make anyone happy. Money can only be associated with the word power. I am not saying that money is not important; I am just trying to bring to the attention of all that money need not be our priority in life.

To walk in a park or beach is free. To sit and dream is free. To pray is free. To believe and choose to share one day a week with those we love is free. We are a people who need to feel the freedom of releasing money as our God as we have placed Him on the back burner of life.

There is no one to compare to us or for us to compare one to another, for as unique individuals we have the ability to think and speak our own thoughts. To reason and plan to choose what we desire. To feel emotion from crying to even laughing. Yet, the birds in the sky that fly from tree to tree are happier than us. They live the life bestowed on them as birds. They are a gift of the miracle to us to remember Him. Where do the birds come from, we could ask. They are the little part of life that once we notice them we can nourish our souls by becoming aware of the simplicity of life that surrounds us all.

Let those you love find their way in life for like the birds we all have our own inner compass. Support and encourage their needs and dreams. To criticize is to inflict pain on yourself and them. You must learn to accomplish to see with your heart. Picture your heart pumping love through your veins. This love is our gift to live a happy, good life by loving all. When was the last time you felt filled with this joy that your life was the best? Did you ever feel this way since becoming an adult? Adults become cynical and calculating as they choose to be too busy to feel their own hearts filling with love.

I have learned to just sit and watch the sun rise and set in a day and to watch a dog playing in the snow as he buries his nose. I can dream today of a sunny beach that warms my soul on a cold winter's day. I rest my brain every day and refresh my soul. You too are capable of doing the same. All of these bring love through my heart. Imagine that love as it is pumping through your veins instead of blood. How exuberant that love will feel inside of you. To be filled with our heart pumping us with love is to believe.

Laughter and tears are opposites, yet we laugh sometimes from nervousness and other times because we are happy. Tears can also be shed when we are sad or happy. Tears of joy are the best feeling you can experience. A feeling like this can be filled with amazement and disbelief as they fall down your face. How happy you will feel at the moment that a tear can be shed. A baby's birth is a joyous occasion which can bring tears of joy for all. A wedding day brings tears of joy that are filled with the pride and love that tomorrow is sure to bring happiness. Think of the many experiences you have shed tears of joy for because you were filled with love. Love is the glue in life.

I myself shed many tears years ago for the need of desiring love in my life. I felt unloved and I was not able to understand that I was not alone. Gracie felt also that she was unloved until the end of her life when she accepted my own love for her. I wonder as I look back if Gracie was aware of her own strengths and capabilities. Today I have learned that because Gracie was my mother, and I her daughter, I am able to change and grow only because Gracie herself accepted her life and what a lesson that was for me.

I have the unique experience of learning through my life that when I believed I was not loved I was fearful, sad, angry, and lost. Scattered in my thinking and feeling process, I began numbing myself by eating the wrong foods as I searched for protection. I always felt this need to have someone to take care of me that was a constant ache in my heart. I simply needed to love myself first to build up my own self-esteem. My choice to travel farther and farther away from my dreams finally ended because I chose to seek in accomplishing love. Love is more than just glue in the existence of my life. It has made for me a happy fulfilling life to be lived. In choosing love I brought kindness to all that cross my path. It is the ability of kindness to nourish and comfort troubled souls. It is this mere act of kindness that let me find myself.

For some it can be uplifting and very rewarding once they try it. The first step to nourishing your soul and believing in yourself needs to start with you. Try to be kind to yourself first to feel the warmth and glow from this act. Once you are gentle and kind to yourself, you will take a step forward without even realizing it towards little acts of kindness to others.

Sadly, society is afraid of the one word that can comfort them and fill them with love. The mention of a little three-letter word fills some with fear and their face muscles tighten as they raise their eyebrows. I myself have been witness to the change in all that I share the word "G O D" with. We are a society that prides itself on the ability to make money, yet we choose to believe that only those who are mentally ill speak of God. Gracie spoke of God and believed in love and she was institutionalized most of her adult life. Had she been loved and more informed she would have been a leader in the world of spirituality. She stumbled and fell, becoming a victim to the belief of all that had been of her generation.

I have questions to ask and answers to seek for tomorrow's generation. How many people do you know who are in such a state that they cannot comprehend those who truly love them and are afraid of themselves filling with love? To love all and try to understand and support one another with no conflict whatsoever is pure love. When anyone is filled with this need to release what is for a chance to change and feel connected, then this person is finding who they are destined to be. No one is ever alone; we just need to believe this which in the end reflects the inner need to change. The love we need to seek is for ourselves. This love dawns on you first when you can accept and love who you are because you are created by God as He saw fit. Everyone cannot be a movie star or model, but we are just as great once we choose to love who we are. Society has drilled into us that the only beautiful people are up on the big screen and in the glamorous magazines.

The person who is truly beautiful is the person who finds love within. No one has the power to take away the strength of another's beauty, yet we choose daily to submit our beliefs that we are not accepted by others and for who we are. Once we learn to erase our disbelief, love, and approval of who we are, then we will see beauty everywhere. Why is this so hard for us to accomplish? Why do we willingly inflict pain on ourselves as well as believe that others know what is best for us and how we should look, act, and be?

With love finally for yourself you will care enough to nourish and respect your own body. There are many early aspects in life that change a beautiful, innocent baby into a loveless, painful, needy, critical adult. We forget our dreams; we forget to love, and we believe others know something we cannot comprehend about ourselves. We choose to give our power in life away to others. Monetary values and possessions become the source of life. Success becomes our goals. Who gets to the top of the mountain first is very important. No matter how difficult, painful, time consuming, and guilty you become, it is important to obtain your goals.

I am not saying to not work hard and reward ourselves with pleasurable objects that money can buy. It is important to believe in love which is free. We can have expensive cars, clothes, jewelry, and houses filled with the best of everything to tell the world of our wealth. All of these material necessities do bring joy and balance into our daily existence. The desire for money and objects bought with the money is not meant to be a matter of life or death. Our abundance is because of belief and the power of our own thought and then we can purchase anything that we feel is satisfying for us in our lives. However, what is not acceptable is pain inflicted on us or others because we have money or we do not. Anger, lying, stealing, cheating, and abuse whether mentally or physically are not love. Only love fills us with the wealth that can nourish our souls.

To create and follow a path that matters to us in our life experience we must be happy. That which puts a smile on your lips and a giggle in your throat creates a world that fills you with joy – when we love ourselves and in turn what we do in life completes our reason for living and we have accomplished sharing that which is important to us. This love I am talking about is pure white and glows brightly as it takes your breath away. Everything we see, hear, and feel is love. With this kind of experience in your daily life you have no fear, pain, sorrow, or worries. The only way to find this love is to first look at yourself and love this person you are, no matter what others, society, or your own thoughts have drilled into your brain.

As you have read in Book One, "The Mansions of the Mind," I am a daughter of a mentally ill woman, Gracie, who has returned home to God a short time ago. I lived my life dedicated to her because I loved her. That is the simple and honest fact of my life with

Gracie. My father, a man who had no clue of the damage he inflicted on another because he chose to believe this was what was expected of him, obviously by what he experienced growing up, lived his life filled with fear and refusing to change and grow.

Once I became a mother, I followed the voice of my heart and held on tightly to the children I loved so that they would prosper and live fulfilling lives empty of any fear that I could have passed on to them. The husband at my side was the greatest teacher one can ask for in life. I chose for many years to believe I had a job to do as a mother and I needed stability and strength to be true to these children. For me, at that time I created balance in my life by focusing on that which brought me joy and strength.

In the end I learned that just like my father, who I was unable to learn and accept knowledge from, I married my husband who taught me what I needed to know. These two men were teachers for me on my path in life. My husband has been able to accept me and let me travel to worlds one only dreams of. May the men of tomorrow learn from these two examples that life is about loving unconditionally and being kind to those you say you love. The word abuse I hope one day is removed from our language and replaced with the word kindness, for I see how difficult it is for people to be kind to one another on a daily basis.

My story that has poured from my fingertips is about love and the life that God has bestowed on all of us. We are all guilty of stepping one foot in front of the other and accepting what we are told. We as a people, men and women, must believe in ourselves to truly live fulfilling lives and learn from the lessons we each offer one another. This is not about religion or belief as much as it is about love. I believe "Love" is the only religion we need to accept into our lives.

In Book Two, "The Passions of the Mind," I shared with you the power of thought that can move mountains. I am proof of the changes that one can accomplish. The bottom belief and foundation of my own life was always to be kind and love all. In admitting to you, the reader, that I struggled with doubt and disbelief I was able to eventually find belief. I am at the end of my story, and I feel sad all over again, as I say "goodbye" to Gracie one more time. To look back on the lifetime we shared and create this story fills me and my soul completely.

The mere fact that I changed drastically from the woman I had been to the woman I am now is proof that there is a process and a path we need to search for. In learning to trust the process and life and believe in myself, I have been able today to tell you this story. Please believe me when I tell you now that ten years ago I would never have been able to share these words with you. The only reason that I can today is because I love myself.

I leave you today with one question, and I hope that your answer is an honest one that comforts your soul and allows you to believe as I do that anything is possible now: "Do you believe that you are a Spiritual Being – a Bearer of Light?" I do!

My Final Bow

I am warmed by the strength of the sun
As the water silently flows by while I write
The stillness of the cool crisp air blows the trees
In the breeze which makes me fill with insight
The beauty of this day for me is the
Awareness of life I am constantly filled with
The desire to accept the knowledge I possess
Creates a need within to nourish my soul
To be filled with love and wonder of tomorrow
Only makes me today crave the future
To be aware of the moment I am in
Fills me with more than delight
God has beckoned me by erasing
The many fears of yesterday
I can no longer recollect
The old pain from days gone by
A haze fills my mind
Even if I struggle to try
The call, the path, or simply the change
Has brought me to this page
What I accomplish now stems
From my own creative stage
At first I was filled with confusion
To believe I was a new me
I wondered what had happened to the old me
That I could no longer see
A cleansing of an entire life
Placed me where I am now
In the end I will stand after all with my
Dreams fulfilled and take my final bow.

The Beginning

About the Author

Linda Amato is a Certified Holistic Health Counselor, Reiki Master and Metaphysical Practitioner. She is a Wife, Mom and Grandmother and very excited about life and her belief that anything is possible.

An avid reader, writer of poetry and journaling, she was led to share this book about life and love as she has experienced it while working with women while they journey into their love of self and Plan "B" of their lives.

She can be reached at: LA@MakingBelievers.com